Free to Be Human

Free to Be Human

EUGENE KENNEDY

IMAGE BOOKS
A DIVISION OF DOUBLEDAY & COMPANY, INC.
GARDEN CITY, NEW YORK
1987

Image Books edition published March 1987 by special arrangement with The Thomas More Press.

Library of Congress Cataloging-in-Publication Data

Kennedy, Eugene C.
Free to be human.

Reprint. Originally published: Chicago: Thomas More Press, © 1979.
    1. Christian life—Catholic authors. 2. Conduct of life.
    3. Emotions—Religious aspects—Christianity.
    4. Self-acceptance—Religious aspects—Christianity.
    5. Happiness—Religious aspects—Christianity. I. Title.
[BX2350.2.K458 1987]   158'.1   86-20935
ISBN 0-385-23539-9 (pbk.)

For Katharine
  Who has always been free
  to be human

Contents

8 *Contents*

Introduction

Being human seems, to many persons, a bad break. It is the very thing they want to get away from, the mixed inheritance they would disown, a kind of a jail from which they would break free. It takes a long time to discover that the human situation is neither prison nor illness, and that attempts to escape it or to cure it disappoint and frustrate us bitterly.

Being human, an ancient phrase tells us, is a condition; it is not, therefore, an obstacle to fulfillment but rather the combination of factors, as seemingly ill-matched as sun and rain, that are just right for growth. We damage ourselves when we think that freedom resides in overcoming, either by force of the will or by gimmickry, the imperfect but dependable truths about our human nature.

Freedom lies somewhere else and, although the road may seem difficult, it leads to a place of endless wonder and refreshment. It brings us home, to the place we have been trying to get to all our lives, back to our origins, where we have no need for pretense, where, as in all true homes, we can be ourselves. "Freedom," Albert Camus wrote, "is nothing else but a chance to be better." That is what most

men and women want, no matter how distorted or disfigured their search for it may become. Beneath it all, they
want to do the right thing, not by coercion but freely; they
want to do the human thing, but they have somehow lost
their way and cannot seem to find it again.

This is a collection of essays on being human, each written with a simple belief that if you give people enough
room and sufficient light, they will make their way to the
truth of themselves. Nobody does that overnight or on a
weekend; the freedom to be human is achieved slowly,
sometimes painfully, and never without a sense of humor.
Our success in making purchase of such freedom depends
on our readiness to enter into our experience—to suffer it as
well as to celebrate it—and always to call it by its right
name. We need a little space on which to stand in order to
do this, for this space offers us perspective on ourselves and
our lives. It enables us to see meaning in what otherwise
might seem only the blur and jumble of everyday events.
We need a place in which we can catch our breath, all too
often lost by strenuous contemporary exercises through
which we hope to escape human nature and its confines.
We need to open our eyes, too often closed in an agonized
mental pursuit of a world that is not our own, so that we
can look into the depths of the mystery, more glorious because of its flaws, in which we are caught up every day.

We miss the human situation when we try to break away
from it. We discover that we can both inhabit and, in a
sense, own our world when we are free enough to face and
actively accept it. The world comes to us freely when we
are free enough to receive it. What is mysterious, Einstein
once wrote, is the source of all art and all science, the
source of all the right questions. Free enough to see our
lives plainly, we discover the wondrous edgings of all that

is truly human about ourselves and others. And we become freer still, perhaps because we forgive ourselves more readily for our humanity; perhaps because we no longer need to apologize or feel ashamed that we are not gods and no longer need strive to be.

Freedom is not what we expected it to be, but it feels familiar and it feels right. Its nature is the opposite of our suppositions, for it is delivered to those who can accept limitations and loss, not as the bloodied curses of a dying universe but as the elements that are mingled with lasting love and the deepest feelings of peace. This book is meant to provide places on the journey where readers can catch their breath and look freshly at things, where they can feel free to be human.

Eugene Kennedy

CHAPTER 1

The New Freedom

A strange new discovery is being made, one that will startle and excite many people. After a century of meditating on all the factors that challenge or diminish our personal choices in life, after the heyday of sensual surrender, people are discovering a marvelous new prospect in their lives —freedom.

This will surely strike many as an almost incredible return to ideas that we have long considered dead and buried by science. The generation that has described itself as being trapped is suddenly aware that it has set many of these snares for itself. Of all things, people are finding out that they can still make choices about their lives and that they can do something about problems and situations which they formerly classified as terminal diseases of living.

There are those who do not use their abilities fully but say that it is the fault of others who do not recognize or encourage them. There can be truth in this, of course, because jealousy can surely kill the possibility of growth. And yet it is also convenient to have people to blame for the fact that we do not use all our energy or that we have lost touch with a passion for life. We sometimes do not become ourselves because saying yes to that involves us in a long series of hard challenges—and harder work—that we would just as soon escape. It meets our own needs not to be more than we are at times; but what a terrible thing to live with this chosen sadness!

Some of us resist growing up because there are rewards to prolonged adolescence that justify not making fuller and freer choices about our existence; this keeps us at a tentative stage of commitment about ourselves, our work, and the other persons in our lives. We may stand back from freedom because we realize just how much it demands of us. And so childhood looks better.

That is why in Joseph Heller's *Something Happened*, the strange passive narrator—a classic example of a modern person refusing adult freedom—proposes that when he grows up he would like "to be a little boy." One can smile at Teddy Roosevelt's post–White House statement as he left for a hunting trip in Africa, "This is my last chance to be a boy again," but making this a life-style for ourselves denies us the fullness of adult experience. That is a terrible fate to choose, the eternal adolescence in which people never understand what life is all about.

There may be situations in which people just shrug their shoulders and let themselves go, saying, in effect, the hell with it. This sometimes happens in regard to excessive eating, drinking, or some other self-defeating maneuver that they know they should do something about but which they stop fighting. Some people prefer living in a messy environment because if they really began to clean things up and put things in order, they would find truths that had been conveniently obscured by the junk they had allowed to pile up all around them.

Other people spend their lives waiting for something to happen to them. They don't do anything because they adopt the Micawber outlook, feeling that some solution to their difficulties will eventually appear like a saving rain on the horizon of their lives. Not much happens for people who wait for fate or wealthy relatives to solve their problems. Many people, however, do live this way, in vague anticipation that things will get better and that somebody or something will come along to rescue them from their difficulties. When we sense that we are responsible for our lives, we know that we fashion much of our own fruitless expectation. We have to make good things happen both for ourselves and others.

Yes, but isn't the human situation bound to be flawed, and don't we have to settle for less? One would not argue with the imperfection of our situation as human beings. It is that very imperfection, however, which means that we are open-ended to change. Were we otherwise—locked into some predetermined plan—we would have no possibilities at all. We all know, if we can admit it, that we could be better, that we could be different in some ways, and that we could do it without hurting people around us.

We can choose to become more loving and more responsive to our neighbor by deciding to be that way in relationship to ourselves. We may not become one hundred percent different, but in the affairs of human growth, a little progress represents a great deal of progress. Nothing just happens to us when we have once again laid hold of our freedom—not fate, middle age, nor the dark at the edge of retirement. We retain our choices to define ourselves and to make of our lives what we want them to be.

Many people go through life like the children in Charles Dickens' books, always looking over their shoulder at some pursuing fate that ever threatens to destroy their happiness. They feel vaguely uneasy about their existence and they are not sure that they can outrun the storm clouds. They always feel that, no matter what good they have accomplished or what noble plans lie before them, something bad is about to happen to them. It doesn't even really have to happen in order to make them feel that way; they keep expecting it the way pessimists keep predicting rain on a cloudless picnic day.

Other people never feel very comfortable in their own estimation. They are, as far as they can see, always falling short or never quite making it in the way they wish. They imagine that they are in competition with some indefinable and elusive ideal that keeps lapping them on the track of life. Still others feel oppressed by the weight of cultural expectations. How, after all, can one keep up with the modern world and all that it frothily expects of people when everything goes so quickly out of style? Last month you were supposed to look like Gatsby and now we are told that the fifties look is in again. Styles affect far more than clothes, of course, and it is not surprising that people should be bewildered or depressed by feeling that they can't keep up with the times, much less with their next-door neighbors.

CHAPTER 2

————————⬥————————

What Do You Say When You Don't Know What to Say?

What can any of us say in those moments that seem to be beyond words, those times, for example, of grief or parting when the heaving of the heart would register on any close-by seismograph but cannot or will not be translated into even the simplest of phrases? What can we say to the sick or the lonely or those struck almost dumb by sorrow? How can we speak to those who mourn and who, in a passage that is silent and elusive, seem beyond our power to contact, traveling in a sphere that neither we nor the best of our words can touch? There is a double suffering here, for even if we could find the words, the very right words for the moment, they would be spoken to hearts too numb to receive them.

We have a betraying collection of responses, second and third best, all of them, for the broken moments of life. We sometimes want to avoid them and to find excuses not to be with those who are ill or grieving, to avoid the pressure of meetings in which we do not know what to say or in which the change in those we know and love seems beyond bearing. We know we must go, and we want in some way to transcend the perfunctory in carrying out the ritual, but most of us are awkward as we enter the sickroom or the funeral parlor or the now-quiet homes of the lonely.

The strange truth is that we need not say much at all and that, if we have faced the pain and want somehow to enter into it—if, in other words, our hearts are full—then something strong and comforting will spill out anyway. Overcoming the first temptation to look away—this is the test for the comfortable who are challenged to bring comfort to others. It is a lesson that simple people teach us all the time.

By "simple" I do not mean the unlettered. The simple people of this earth are the uncomplicated ones, those in whose lives there is a wholeness, a way of seeing connections and relationships that is not given to the oversophisticated. The simple people are a source of grace because they are direct in their responses. They see the needs of others clearly and do not let themselves get in the way as they reach out to them.

Watch old friends embrace wordlessly at a moment of intense meaning, at a time of joy or sorrow, at a rich cross-section of existence where the finely honed strength of experience can be communicated fully and in an instant. Watch a mother with a sick child or a loving husband and wife under the same storm of grief. They may not know what to say but they instinctively know what to do. An old secret this, the treasure of unaffected presence, a continuing share in the mystery of revelation, a hint about the power of the presence in which all our loves are set.

How strange the very idea of saying nothing seems in a world bobbing on a milky wash of talk, a world, indeed, in which communication is celebrated as a near sacrament, and in which telling everything, every last slightly soiled detail, has become the password to redemption in a confessional universe. How unsporting it seems to say nothing when the grinding mills of our public curiosity chop, as noisily as a ravenous hound, at whatever scraps and tidbits of gossip and rumor that can be fed to them. How unfair not to tell what you know about yourself or about others, especially the famous, if you have had a privileged look at them. The public's right to know—yes, of course, how could we have forgotten? We forget that this shaggy maxim is balanced by the private person's right to remain silent. We forget the mystery of silence and our profound need for it as a condition for our psychological and moral maturity.

It is not just the silence that is filled with meaning when we open our hearts quietly to somebody else, although that raises an edge of the mystery and lets us sense how charged with power silence can be when people are listening to each other's depths. Silence is not just a discipline for monasteries and library reading rooms, not a regulation demanded to safeguard others from distractions. Silence is not a void but a world of its own. Modern persons will never get in touch with themselves with a transistor radio plugged into their ears. And the crackle of CB radios won't help much either. Silence is a choice, not a penance, an opportunity for deepening one's identity when it is used, for example, for study or serious work or for meditation and prayer. How could we ever really hear the world whispering its concerns to us unless we listened in silence for a while?

There is a silence that matches our best possibilities when we have learned to listen truly to others, to receive them into ourselves in the active listening that depends on our mastering the lessons of being quiet within ourselves, of stilling the swelling sea of our own concerns in order to be able to hear clearly what someone else is saying. This is vital for friends and lovers, for parents with their children, and teachers with their students. We need to cut off the garbled static of our own preoccupations and our own urges to give short-cut solutions to people who want something simpler and yet grander—our quiet attention.

And there are times when there is nothing to say, nothing that could fit the occasion. There are times when silence is the most sacred of responses. It is not a sin, for example, to allow intervals of silence during religious services; we need those silences for the work of consolidating the resources of our spirits, to let the truths of faith sink in more deeply. We need such moments to hear God speak to us.

And there are other times when our wordy clichés break like brittle swords in frozen weather. That is why, as Emily Dickinson once wrote, there is a hush in a home on the morning after death, a silence that would be violated by too many words. There are times in which silence is our place of communion rather than estrangement, when we are caught up in the same loss or difficulty or misunderstanding.

Even those who love each other very deeply must master the lesson of silence and its meaning in their relationship. There are moments—after hurt, intended or not, for example—when only silence will do. Is it too great a gift to ask, too much respect for the way things heal, to expect silence when saying something, saying anything at all, only makes things worse? Remaining silent even when one longs to apologize and buy release from the pain or tension of wounding a loved one: This is as hard a discipline as we know, and how hard it is for any of us to master it. But it is in silence that love speaks softly; it is in such sacrificial silences that forgiveness finds its voice.

CHAPTER 3

Security Versus Satisfaction

People who save too much, both of their things and of themselves, may overemphasize security so much that they deprive themselves of satisfaction. They cannot, in other words, even enjoy what should be the legitimate fruits of their careful living. This is a feature of the overly obsessive personality who bends his or her back too much to overemphasized duty. This is not to criticize duty nor to indict all obsessive features in the human personality. A little obsessiveness, however, goes a long way. Its grip is steel and once closed over souls, it does not loosen easily; the obsessive life-style can lock us outside of life. Only life experienced in some depth—always the chance that it may be over our heads—delivers satisfaction, a sign as good as any we are likely to get that we are spending ourselves wisely.

Persons who want too much security live as though someone were watching them and making notes on every small move, underlining the mistakes and readying a terrible judgment for any failure to be perfect. It also means that an individual may hide away the best parts of himself or herself because it is too uncertain to be exposed to the risks of living closely with other human beings. There is a perennial tension between our desire to be with others and our tendency to withdraw into a saving isolation where no one can get close enough to hurt us. When a passion for security makes love even harder than it ordinarily is in life, there is clearly something wrong, something that needs inspection and treatment before terminal bitterness sets in.

Another penalty connected with the excessive desire for security is that it squeezes all the enjoyment out of life. The obsessive approach to everything puts a liability on the legitimate and wonderful reactions that go along with a freer style of life. Mid-life becomes difficult for persons who bet everything on security because they come to realize that the payoff is not as great as they had hoped, that, for all their saving and scrimping and carefulness, they are not getting ahead or being recognized in the way they had dreamed. They have saved and slaved and it has not worked; it is small wonder that they feel betrayed and depressed. The saddest part is that they don't know why and that they cannot find their way back to start.

Father Theodore Hesburgh of Notre Dame once hypothetically inquired: "What would be important to us if we suffered a sudden great calamity or disaster? Where would we want to be and with whom would we want to be?" This science-fiction scenario would, he suggested, allow us to discover something about what we really believe in, care about, and what we really build our lives on. It is a good cue to the imagination, sparking us to take a long and thoughtful look at our lives and their goals.

The question opens a door that may lead conscientious adults to a scene of comfort rather than regret. At the present moment, in many different kinds of lives, grown-ups are wondering if all the sacrifices they have made on behalf of their children or in serving others have really been worthwhile. This is a classic mid-life or mid-career concern, especially when the results or the critical judgments of the supposedly sophisticated make us unsure about whether or not we have made the right bets in life. Many parents, for example, are surprised and dismayed to hear social critics indict the late forties and fifties as a near-medieval period in which the idea of keeping marriages and families together was almost naively accepted. Did we work too hard at something we really believed in, only to find now that we are considered foolish for it? This type of inquiry is not uncommon these days, and it is not just a theoretical debate. It is further complicated for parents who see their children take positions that estrange them from their own values. Such persons need some reassurance about their lives, some confidence that, if they have put other persons first and have tried to make genuine love work despite all the obstacles that were thrown in its way, they have not invested themselves unwisely. Any effort to live unselfishly causes us to experience pain, but because it breaks us open to each other, it makes joy a lasting and incorruptible possession, something that outlasts the faddish critics of the day.

Genuinely entitled to regrets are the persons who approach life in the style of a miser, keeping their treasures, as poet John Milton once wrote, in "unsunn'd heaps." It is not just fortune they bury away, it is something of themselves, something they are saving for a better day and a surer opportunity for success in human relationships. Such people have, in Shakespeare's phrase, only winter for their bounty; they never harvest or share because they are so focused on saving themselves. They never give enough of themselves to others even to feel a genuine disappointment of the heart later in life. They can only know the haunting feeling that comes from emptiness, the cold, damp isolation of the dungeon they have built for themselves. It is true of these people that, although they save things, they never really invest them. Truly, they miss not just something but everything that is important in life. It is also sad for these persons to discover that, in rueful moments like those of the old actor in O'Neill's play, they may discover that some of the things they packed into their double-locked treasure chests as gold are only brass.

CHAPTER 4

Magnificent Obsession

Obsessive compulsiveness has been called the classic American psychological difficulty, one that helped to build the country, solve its problems, and continues to make it difficult for its citizens to enjoy their accomplishments. The middle generation of Americans seem to prove this point: They are obsessed with finding quick, pragmatic solutions for every challenge, from friendship to the energy crisis; they labor so hard at their leisure-time activities that they turn them into work, thus draining the zest from what should refresh them. The obsessive approach to life seems to guarantee that we will get things done; sometimes, however, we do not understand fully what we have achieved through our head-down, self-denying concentration. We drop an atom bomb or land on the moon ahead of schedule and only then confront the implications of these feats. Americans shake their heads and say, "There has to be more to life than practice, practice, practice, and work, work, work, but what is it? And how do you achieve it?" This is the constant question of a generation of achievers who are still tangled in the strands of the Puritan ethic.

Obsessions are generally defined as thoughts that recur even though they are unwanted. These intrusions, which frequently invade people's minds at inappropriate moments —as, for example, during religious services—cannot be willed away. They cannot be excluded from our minds, and the harder we try, the more they stand like irate tenants resisting eviction. These obsessions may come in the form of an individual thought or some frightening or unpleasant word; they can also clothe themselves more elaborately as obsessive ruminations. The individual cannot shake off a certain subject, some personal difficulty, or perhaps even a theoretical notion; these keep coming into the imagination like waves sweeping endlessly onto the shore. The problem is that, despite the rumination, there is never any conclusion; the tide never lowers to offer relief to the individual.

Frequently, obsessions of this sort are concerned with doubts or indecision about some important or unimportant situation. Did I, the person asks, do the right thing? Or, they ask over and over again, is this the right thing to do? A variant reading poses the inquiry: Could I or should I have done differently? These doubts and indecisions seem to hound the person without ever resolving themselves.

It is important to distinguish these obsessive clouds of thought from the ordinary business of being preoccupied about some important matter. It is perfectly normal for individuals to find that the issues involving a particular decision or forthcoming event absorb a great deal of their attention. These usually concern something that is in the process of being resolved, however, and the concern is a measure of the importance of the situation. People can usually put these aside without great effort in order to concentrate on other business of the moment. The classic obsessive thought is unwelcome; it is uninvited and hard to dismiss.

It does not follow, of course, that all unwelcome thoughts are obsessive. We may on any given day have many unwelcome thoughts that surprise and dismay us. We can turn away from them without finding them riding our

backs through every conscious moment. It is also quite understandable that these thoughts come to human beings.
There is nothing wrong, nothing evil in itself about the
notions and fantasies that may arise in the healthiest of
human imaginations.

Sometimes people experience obsessions because they
are afraid of something they might do. They fear, for example, that they may hurt some member of their family. The
wife may truly be afraid that she is going to do something
in the preparation of the meals that may poison the other
members of the family. She goes to great lengths to avoid
this, sometimes insisting that someone else be present with
her when she prepares food, or relinquishing this important
function out of fear of what she may do in the midst of it.
The same kind of obsession can bother a husband, who
may be afraid of his own impulses to harm members of his
family. It is not that these people are likely to act out these
impulses but they are very frightening in themselves, so
people go to great lengths to avoid the fear that comes to
them when these obsessions are present. Obviously, obsessions of this kind can interfere with the person's healthy
functioning in life.

So, too, it is with the first cousins to obsessions, the compulsions. As the obsessions concern thoughts, compulsions
are concerned with actions. Some psychiatrists describe
compulsion as an obsession in action because the psychological mechanisms are so similar. Compulsions may concern a single kind of activity, such as the classic one of
touching all the posts in a fence on the way home, stepping
on all the cracks in the sidewalk, or washing one's hands
over and over again. A person may not be able to operate
unless a certain set of actions is performed in a certain way,

whether this involves organizing a desk or packing a suitcase.

Religious scrupulosity—repeating prayers over and over again—is a classic example of this compulsive behavior. Compulsion is also seen in individuals who must constantly check over what they have already checked thoroughly. This includes things like putting out lights, turning off ranges, and checking to see that the baby is all right. It is found in the individual who cannot seem to finish an essay or some other assignment. Such a person starts, may write a few paragraphs or a few pages, but then tears it up and starts over again. People acting on their compulsions are great starters but they are not very good at finishing things. It is a problem filled with a special kind of suffering.

It is important to note that in serious cases these compulsive rituals are very important to the person's adjustment. Afflicted individuals become very upset if we interfere with them or try to get them to stop or to carry things out in a different way. What drives us crazy about these people turns out to be the thing that is helping to keep them sane.

The presence of obsessive-compulsive problems challenges our willingness to listen carefully, with sensitive understanding, to the behavior of other persons. We must get beneath the surface, to the core that alone can explain what we observe externally. This is not the place to treat either ourselves or others superficially or amateurishly. The presence of obsessive-compulsive symptoms is a way we have of talking to ourselves and a way of saying something about ourselves to others. It is a symbolic way of saying, "This is the best I can do to deal with what is going on inside me. It is not to be taken at face value; the meaning is deeper." We are saying, in effect, "I have a conflict and this is the only way I can handle it."

There are, of course, traces of obsessive-compulsive behavior in almost everybody. This is nothing to be alarmed by. In fact, a little obsessive-compulsive behavior is very functional in helping us to get things done, to finish what we begin, and to be careful in carrying out our responsibilities. We are not talking about this milder form of obsessive concern as much as about the exaggerations of the condition, which can interfere with our life and with our happiness. It is not self-indulgence to learn as much as we can so that we can do something constructive, if possible, about the problem.

The conflict beneath these symptoms is generally described as being between authority and control. A great deal of unexpressed anger frequently bubbles beneath such conflict; this is the classic anger that cannot be faced in a direct way. Some observers style the obsessive's conflict as being between obedience and defiance, with the basic question being: Shall I be good or may I have permission to be bad? It is a condition filled with opposites and contradictions. In these we get some feeling for the underlying conflict as well as for the hostile elements that are characteristically present. Obsessive persons handle a conflict that is below the level of consciousness in the only way that is available to them at the moment. It is not pleasant for them, especially when, as often happens, they recognize intellectually the nature of their difficulty. One of their problems is that they tend to treat themselves on this intellectual level, talking about the problem, rationalizing it in the worrisome way that is practically the hallmark of the difficulty itself. They find it hard to feel the conflict—to let themselves feel its dimensions—because this would be too threatening. We can be understanding and responsive— even forgiving of ourselves—when we get some sense of the fact that this behavior is an outer translation of inner problems.

The sad part about the obsessive approach to life is that it makes people want to get things right in such a distorted way that their dutifulness leaves no margin for any enjoyment. They attempt to wall out the risk of living with the bricks of obsessiveness. One of the problems is that all their efforts to get the tiny pieces of experience together prevent them from ever seeing it whole. This is often compounded when their carefully prepared plans do not work out. What they thought they had covered proves to be elusive after all. As a result they can only react with depression, by getting mad inside themselves and thus further denying themselves even a minimal experience of deep joy and happiness. It is no fun adjusting to life this way, and these people, as much as any other group in our society, deserve a liberation of their personalities so that they may more freely and fully experience themselves and the meaning of their own lives.

It doesn't do any good to get mad at ourselves, to try to talk ourselves out of our obsessions, or to make repeated acts of the will that are designed to send them into exile. That doesn't work with ourselves and it surely does not work with others. It is sad to see that these are sometimes the courses of action that people use. They try to fight fire with fire, but this merely intensifies the inner problem. Nor is this the kind of difficulty we can solve with the glib but reasonable advice to take a vacation, develop another interest, or take up golf. These activities merely become substitute occasions for obsessive and compulsive behavior. If you don't believe me, take a look at the obsessive way in which some people handle their hobbies or their golf game. Burdened with duty, they end up no closer to enjoyment than they were before. Their attempted pleasure has turned and devoured them.

Reason is not the first course of action in dealing with this problem in either its mild or more aggravated form. Reason simply plays into the whole defensive pattern where words are used to control emotions and where it is much easier to think about oneself than to feel one's experience. The obsessive approach is filled with rational doubting; this, as the old cliché goes, is indeed the name of the game. It is essentially an emotional problem of which complicated rationality is a feature.

It helps very much to approach the problem with some humility, a readiness to listen, and a recognition that the symptoms are not in themselves the problem. Symptoms say that something is going on, that there is a psychological conflict that needs to be brought to the surface. This involves listening to our feelings and allowing them to come into our consciousness without being frightened off by them. Sometimes we need to have the help of somebody else to cope with them effectively. Sometimes we are the ones asked to give that kind of help. We do not punish nor do we attack these defenses, but we do try to respond to the whole person with a conviction that redemption is possible—and here a little progress is a lot of progress—if we can be acceptant, understanding, and forgiving.

It helps to understand the human condition and the complicated way in which we signal our internal difficulties through these external signs. It makes us more patient with ourselves. In the space that this patience creates we may be able to reevaluate the goals of our lives and to check off those activities that are nonproductive or not constructive for our human growth and spiritual development. We can, with compassion for ourselves and others, allow ourselves to explore our own conflicts more freely, to loosen up in our way of looking at ourselves and the expectations we place on life.

Balancing our need for security a little less tightly against our freedom to enjoy life's satisfactions seems a small step, but in reality it is quite a large one. It means that we can believe in ourselves even though we are imperfect, that we still see our possibilities, and that life does not have to be met like a note on demand. This is the same attitude that practical faith enables us to have toward others. It is not the least of gifts to believe in others and so to liberate them from this special, sad imprisonment of obsessive and un-redemptive living. This, indeed, is one of the functions of active believing: to give freedom to others because we commit ourselves to their fuller possibilities. Faith does not fix itself on obsessive involvement with the tiny details of life; it gives a grander and more redemptive vision of ourselves and others. It is this kind of faith that makes us whole.

CHAPTER 5

————◆————

What to Do When You're Feeling Down

Probably no subject has inspired more advice than that malady, more common than the common cold itself, which has many names and no name at all. I mean, of course, that frayed stage curtain which falls unexpectedly and rudely across our day to leave us without enthusiasm, energy, or even much hope. Call it the blues or the blahs; everybody knows what this experience is like, but few of us have learned to cope with it successfully. We usually wait for it to pass, and sooner or later it does; in the meantime we go through the motions of life as best we can. It is like being caught in an airport because of a fog that we can neither pray nor propel away; we just wait in the uncomfortable chairs, a restless and steamy crowd of fellow travelers milling about us, until the overcast lifts away by itself.

But is that all we can do? Not according to those who love to give advice—be it philosophical or physical. ("Try the Canadian Air Force Exercises.") Some of us have tried all of these solutions and ended up wiser, if not less melancholic, for all our exertions. We never feel so good as at the moment when our mood or depression begins to dissipate —"How," we ask ourselves, "did I get over this one?"— thinking if only we could remember this evaporating combination we might apply it earlier the next time. But the reasons why we emerge from the blackness are as hard to identify as the reasons we sink into it. What can a person do?

Well, there are several solutions that we can quickly put aside. These include drinking, daydreaming, and taking drugs. These are popular ways of escaping from the very real pain of being down. However, their distracting or mollifying effects on us are tragically temporary, and when their magic is over we are more depressed than ever—and no closer to understanding why. There is nothing easier to talk oneself into than a couple of quick ones to purge the soul of the day's accumulated dross. Even tranquilizers are socially acceptable in this day when we settle for anything that promises to take the edge off life, even for a few hours.

The first step we might take is to remember that ups and downs are rather normal and they do not generally require drastic medicines or overkill responses. There is something to be said for the Far Eastern method of letting ourselves swim with the tide of life even when it is running against us. Thrashing about blindly may cost us more energy and generate more frustration than it is really worth. In other words, most people have cyclic moods and they should not get too upset when these occur. For the average person, a few moments of self-reflection may help him or her to understand why their emotions have suddenly taken a nose dive. The trouble, of course, is that when we do not feel very well, we do not feel like inspecting our emotions either. That is one of the reasons why a little snag in our day can have such a powerfully depressing effect on us. Let me explain.

Suddenly, overcast emotional weather comes from a rapidly forming front of small hurts or disappointments—a big storm touched off by a lot of little lows in our everyday life. For example, upon rising, a person may feel fairly fit and ready to work energetically all day. At breakfast, however, his wife brings up something that takes the air out of him—like telling him that he is beginning to look middle-aged.

This is a small blow (a little murder, if you will), so glancing that we hardly admit it into our consciousness—hardly, in other words, give a name to it when it occurs. Its effect is nonetheless telling, in part because the nature of this comment is such that we do not like to say, even to ourselves, that such things bother us. Yet deep inside us, these psychological viruses of the human condition continue to sap our strength all day long. To handle these situations adequately we must be willing to trace the path of our depression back to the incident that set it off. This takes time and honesty. It may also require a sense of humor; otherwise we might be appalled at the size or character of the event that laid us low. A good laugh, as we recognize our human frailty, is very therapeutic.

A further suggestion for really getting to the bottom of our bad moods is to try listening to the way in which we talk about our life and hard times to others—whether they are the hairdresser or close friends. Talk out loud to yourself if you must, but be sure to listen carefully—you may catch many hints of what you are really like as a person. You may even be able to siphon off the self-pity that so easily becomes a part of complaining. You will get a better picture of yourself and your own role in your depressions than you could get from a book full of self-help philosophy. And if you listen to yourself long enough, you may begin to smile and then to laugh a little at the inconsistencies of your own position. Before you know it, you will feel much better.

CHAPTER 6

No Has Always Been
a Good Answer

This is the first announcement of the establishment of the Society for the Preservation and Encouragement of Saying No. As a matter of fact, it is probably the only announcement you'll see. Saying no, after all, has been out of fashion for quite some time. Nobody says no very much or very often—not parents to children, teachers to their students, friends or lovers to each other.

Yes is in, not just as an answer, but as a style of life. It is praiseworthy, indeed, to say yes to life, but I wonder if we are ever able to do that without learning how to say no along the way. Learning how to say no may just be indispensable in the healthy affirmation of life.

But yes as a style is connected with the belief that we are entitled to treat ourselves bountifully all the time. "Thou shalt not deny thyself gratification" has been a commandment of the swinging seventies. It has literally been hell on some people to face a period of recession in which they suddenly found life saying no to them. For many it was their first experience of denial or frustration on a major scale; it struck them like a cosmic accident, a phenomenon over which they could exercise no control, a sudden bank of clouds shifting across what they thought were endless blue skies.

Saying yes had been in because we were never supposed to disappoint or frustrate each other's wishes. No was not a viable alternative in an environment in which grabbing all the gusto and squeezing all the pleasure out of existence was the accepted code of the sophisticated life. Well, you can't blame anybody for wanting to scratch through the sometimes dreary surface of life to uncover a measure of happiness.

The thing is that happiness has never been a synonym for pleasure, and fulfillment has never come with being able to get everything we want. No looms up as familiarly in our lives as the rock formations of Monument Valley in a John Wayne Western. No stands there, its sheer face against the sky, defying us to climb it every day. No has the immediate virtue of being clear and concise. It is refreshing in an age when we are tempted to say maybe about so many things. As a matter of fact, we often say maybe with our lips when there is really a no deep down in our hearts.

Think of the trouble we would save if we said no early and opportunely instead of the floundering maybes that go into phrases like "I think so but I'll have to check my calendar first" or "I'm pretty sure I can make it but I'll let you know if anything comes up." Think for a moment of those unanswered invitations, their inner protective tissues still tucked neatly in their folds, to which, somehow, we cannot say no so we end up not saying anything at all, leaving the host and hostess in a distress almost as great as our own.

Think of the occasions we can look back on when we wish we had said no, when we knew very well we should have said no, and, because we didn't, we sank slowly and moodily into some unenjoyable party, event, or business deal.

People think "no" is a negative word, one that closes us off from good chances. Often enough, however, it is quite positive, the symbol of a mature decision that frees us and others of obligations we don't need and shouldn't assume.

Think of the noes we regret not uttering and we have reason to look more kindly on the word. It may be as simple as "I shouldn't have had that dessert" or "I wish I hadn't said that" or "I wish I hadn't done that." Regrets are poor marrow in the soup of existence; they are more anguishing when we look back and understand that we saw a choice and made the wrong decision, that we almost knew it at the time, and yet . . .

Nothing calls back words uttered or deeds accomplished; the heart creaks under the weight of the noes we never spoke. Saying no when we have the chance and the sense that it is the right thing to do may be the beginning of wisdom in life.

Part of the trouble with no lies in resolving the conflict that we want to look away from rather than settle. That is why maybe creeps into our vocabulary. But that just describes the fact that we are in conflict; it is a symptom of our vacillation rather than an effective solution.

Maybe is a deceptive buyer of time. And frequently we only use the interval to sweat and to stew instead of trying to get at the roots of our indecision. Perhaps we would do better if we were less afraid of saying no, if the curse could be purged from the word, and we could feel freer to use it.

The truth is, of course, that there is no way to experience life in depth unless we are ready to say no and have it said to us over and over again. We are supposed to learn early as children that we cannot always have our own way, and still life tries to teach this to us over and over. We are not omnipotent, and there is no magic to free us from the limits of the human situation. We cannot be here and be there, we cannot say yes without also saying and meaning no to some, perhaps many, other things.

It is a strange mystery, learning to say no to ourselves the better to be able to say yes to our best possibilities in life. A hard mystery but full of truth as we sort out our motives and discover that there are many times when we must say no to those we love or accept the no that they speak to us. It is a deep mystery because it tempers our personalities but it does not dull them.

We live in a rushing maw of disappointments, frustrations, and delays, and we survive because we know the lessons that "no" teaches us. We are ringed with the mystery of actively accepting rather than just putting up with the truths that "no" seeds into our lives. It is a mystery, learning to say yes to no, and finding ourselves made whole in the process.

CHAPTER 7

————◆————

The Hardest Thing to Do . . .

Perhaps we should never use the superlative degree, never talk about the best or the worst of anything, never make premature judgments about places, persons, or events because in the human situation we always seem to find a way to top ourselves. But there may be one experience where we can make the claim, one test of the soul that we all recognize as an unsurpassed trial. This, of course, is the cross section of life in which what we are called upon to do is to do nothing.

You can think of many circumstances in which doing nothing is the best but also the hardest thing. It is not just the restraint that is required after an accident when we know we are not supposed to move the injured person until the doctor comes, although the anxiety of wanting to do something and not being able to while the sirens wail in the distance can be very intense. The pressure is even greater in interpersonal situations in which the hurt is invisible and we know that no emergency medic, no angel, even, is hurrying to take over or heal the situation for us.

Sometimes this occurs when there has been a misunderstanding that cannot easily be untangled. Oh, logic and facts suggest an easy and direct solution, but alas, logic and facts cannot ever be warm enough to break up ice floes in the heart. We may have a perfectly rational explanation for

what did or did not happen, but the emotions have a law
unto themselves, and the force of reason seems brittle and
fragile and finally useless by comparison. "Don't say anything . . ." people will warn us, and yet we want to say
something, we want to make a point clear, we want some
settlement, some slight promise of understanding. . . .

The hard truth is that in such an incident the only thing
to do is to do nothing, to wait while the time needed for
healing from inside passes and the misperceptions can be
unscrambled. But can you think of a heavier tax than to
wait quietly in the very moments in which we are anxious
to do something constructive? The need to wait in silence,
to do nothing when every fiber in us cries out to do something, anything, in order to improve things is a real test of
devotion. It is, in fact, a dimension of love about which we
think too little. It takes a great deal of love and patience to
hold ourselves back, to let the emotional storm in someone
close to us blow itself out, before we can get together again.
And yet this happens all the time in life.

We have to learn, if we are going to be truly loving, to
give others room in which to be unreasonable, to let them
express their grief or distress symbolically, to stand back
and not interfere, despite our internal pressures to do so, as
they work through the emotional side of their distress. As a
matter of fact, when we do intervene out of due time, we
frequently make things worse, both for the other person
and for ourselves. Blessed are the peacemakers, for they
have learned how to wait; blessed are they, for they have
learned to understand the complexities of human reactions
and they know the sacred times when doing nothing is
both the hardest and the best thing to do.

CHAPTER 8

━━━━━◆━━━━━

The Last Thing to Grow Old

The very last thing we lose to age, the Greek philosopher tells us, is our capacity for anger; wrath can still flow over the dry plains of old age. Whether that is true or not, anger still has not lost its standing among the evils of the world. At the same time, we speak about—and the Scriptures contain examples of—righteous anger, the legitimate wrath that people experience in the face of injustice or unredeemed cruelty. Our reactions to wrath are mixed indeed.

A person without passion is judged not much of a person at all; we wonder whether an individual who cannot feel strongly can ever love deeply. Love and hate flower from the same roots of personality, and we do not quickly interfere with a person's ability to grow angry lest we commit sacrilege by violating something that is a vital component of his or her human identity.

So, like death and taxes, anger abides—and human beings have never quite figured out exactly how to handle it. People do not want to be swift to anger and they do not believe that impulsive anger is a solution to anything. Not many of us have the heart to say, as the late Huey Long once did, that success in certain political endeavors depends on learning how to hate. We want to see anger in perspective and, if anything, be its master rather than its subject.

Our experience of anger is akin to that of sexuality because both of these qualities of personality have been subjected to so much repression. This does not mean that they are dissolved in the unconscious; rather it suggests that these forces are active even when we are not aware of them. They are aspects of our motives and our interest, reflections of our true selves, sparks that fire our individuality even when we do not directly acknowledge them. That is why some intensely angry people do not recognize their own anger at all; they are like persons living in a house whose basement is filling with steam from overworked boilers while they are still comfortable in the living room, quite unconcerned about the occasional tremble in the floorboards.

Repressed anger does as much mischief on the uninspected side of personality as severely repressed sexuality. Most unadmitted forces that are kept in the dark manage to do us harm. We may not like what we find when we visit the cobwebbed cellar of the self; it is, however, a far safer and more humane thing to do than to ignore what is really taking place in us. It is better to find what is there—whether it is anger, sex, or fear—than to try to live without knowing what moves us.

It has been suggested that much anger is suppressed precisely because we live in a frustrating world in which so little can be done about the things that cause us pain or difficulty. In government, industry, religion, and education, we learn to accommodate ourselves to situations that are wrong but seem, in the final analysis, to be the fault of no specific individual. Causes come together like chemicals flowing toward each other from opposite directions, and few persons can predict the reaction that takes place when they finally mingle. Such uninspected anger is the problem; men and women, if they are to live in relative peace with themselves or with each other, need to face and learn something about their own individual anger. It may be the best preventive psychological medicine they can take.

Learning about our anger generally requires an indirect approach. We have to sneak up on it because most of us do not like to think of ourselves as angry persons. We may admit that we have a short temper or a low boiling point, but that is far different from recognizing more subtle and constant forms of anger. We often avoid admitting these things about ourselves, a maneuver that is perfectly understandable. A little knowledge about our capacity for anger is, however, a lot of knowledge if we want to avoid destroying another or being destroyed by it. The following is a brief checklist on the subject of anger that may help us to understand ourselves and therefore possess ourselves better:

Do we quickly deny anger? Are we, in other words, the first witnesses in our own behalf, and do we protest just a little too much the possibility of our own anger? If we discover that we have a need to deny the presence of anger in ourselves, then we have firsthand evidence that it exists in a way that displeases us and in a form with which we do not want to deal. When our defenses against anger go up swiftly, we can almost be certain that there is something here that needs a closer look. We might begin by asking ourselves why we need to deny something that is such a common human experience.

Are we depressed, feeling down and discontent without being able to account for it? Depression is frequently the reaction to anger that is not being faced or handled straightforwardly. We go on being depressed until we can recognize and admit the anger. You can tell if you are right because of the way depression lifts almost instantly when you are able to call your anger by its right name and identify its source in some conflict in your life.

Are we very hard on ourselves? This is a sign of anger toward something about ourselves. To find ourselves quite displeased with our own personality or our own performance suggests that a deeper and more careful look at our interior life is appropriate. It can save us from raining undeserved blows on our own selves and also open up the possibility of a cheerier and happier life.

Sometimes it is easier to see anger in other persons. One of the symptoms is that bristly attitude, the porcupine syndrome, that makes other people difficult to approach. They are, we say, hostile, and they telegraph their anger so clearly that others stay well away from them. It is all very well to pick up these signals from other persons; at times, however, we might apply this test in reverse. If we notice other people staying at a distance from us or hesitating to bring up subjects to us—in general, treating us like a live bomb that has been discovered in their garden—then it may be time to inspect our own bristles. Whether we admit our anger or not, it clearly affects those around us; reactions from others indicate that it is time for us to do something constructive. This can come with the simple admission that we may be angry at something after all.

If these are indications that we need to inspect our anger more closely, the next step is as important as it is difficult. It is hard to name our anger because it is difficult to get close to it or because, at some level of our consciousness, we have already despaired over doing anything about it. There are also times when it is just too painful to look at situations that generate excessive anger in us. Some of these follow:

The situation may be one which we help to design,

thinking we are doing the right thing at the time, but building incidents that ultimately close down on us. Any person is angry when he finds that the trap in which he lives is one that he helped to construct. One of the most common complaints of the day arises from individuals who feel trapped in their marriage, their job, or in their living situation. Deserting spouse and children—as some have done in these circumstances—is a sign of the frustration and sometimes motivating anger underlying these acts. Divorce or separation proceedings are hardly ever carried out without angry feelings, and many of these are of the trapped variety.

Anger can be associated with major assaults on our life experience. It is quite common for people to react to illness or death with angry feelings. These are human reactions that cannot be prevented and which need not be denied in order to be controlled. It is a shameful thing for people to admit that they are angry at those times when they feel that they should be acceptant of God's will. Nonetheless, anger is almost always present; few people escape major life experiences without at least some feelings of anger. This is characteristic of certain phases of the mourning process, for example, and we should not be surprised at it. We get mad when our life or relationships are suddenly drastically changed and we want to blame somebody else for the turn of events. Sometimes we get mad at doctors—a vulnerable and frequently blameless group—or even at the person who has died for seemingly deserting us. These angers pass when they can be verbalized; they can also fester and do great damage when we refuse to admit them.

Anger frequently rises in individuals when they are going through counseling or psychotherapy. They do not understand it and they frequently do not wish to admit it for the same reasons that we have just discussed. This kind of anger is part of the process of transference which is common in helping relationships. It is one of the things that therapists must understand very sensitively lest they suspect that their patients are genuinely angry with them. Feelings appropriate to other persons and other relationships must come into focus if the psychotherapy or counseling means anything. If an individual's feelings do not get stirred up in one way or another, then it is appropriate to wonder whether anything is going on in a helping relationship of which he or she is a part. To become angry is, in most instances, a sign that a person is coming to terms with inner problems.

Last of all, of course, we must remember that there are sometimes good reasons for getting mad, for letting our passions express themselves in the strength of our convictions and, at times, in the power of our criticism or confrontation. Anger may be appropriate in the face of injustice, unnecessary cruelty, or when major responsibilities have been ignored and other people have been hurt as a result. Sometimes it is healthy to get angry at a person who is not realizing his or her full potential. It does not hurt at times to let people know that their misjudgments or misstatements have consequences. I am not suggesting that we should go around knocking people on the head; there are, however, moments when appropriate anger is justified and when we fail ourselves and others if we do not express it.

This last approach can best be used by individuals who know themselves well enough to avoid being carried away by forces which they later rationalize as justified anger. There is a difference between destructive and constructive anger, between the kind of strength that lives with gentleness and the blind fury that lives only for itself. In any case, there is no need to be angry with ourselves because we have experienced strong feelings. It is a sign that we all belong to the same family, and that we need each other's help and understanding to face up to and deal sensibly with everything that is in us.

CHAPTER 9

A Story to Remember

I recently came across a card that carried a portion of the past with it. It was like opening a long-closed chest to free pungent aromas from forgotten events in the dry, quiet space of an attic.

> With feet to take me where I'd go,
> With eyes to see the sunset's glow,
> With ears to hear what I would know;
> I'm blessed indeed. The world is mine;
> Oh God, forgive me when I whine!

Well, verses like that are not written anymore; maybe we should be grateful and maybe we shouldn't. But there is something worth thinking about here. . . .

This is especially true when we get to feeling sorry for ourselves—and who completely escapes the temptation for any length of time?—or when we seem too discouraged to do further battle with life for a while. That is when we might remember some of the people who are facing things far more difficult than any that challenge us.

Take, for example, Rita and James Walter of New York, whose twenty-three-year-old son Paul was stabbed to death in one of those tragic subway incidents that nobody, no poet or preacher anywhere, can make meaningful. So the District Attorney, in describing the assault by two youths, said, "It could have been anyone. Whoever sat in that seat was never going to get up from that seat again." Paul Walter had been a graduate student in psychology and it was the rush hour. One young man stood in front of him so none of the other passengers could see while the other stabbed him in an effort to get his wallet away.

But Rita and James Walter—would they not be entitled to weep in anger forever?—stood before a judge as one of the accused was about to be sentenced and asked for leniency for him. They had done the same for the other defendant earlier in the year. They favored leniency, they said, because they did not want to see "another life wasted" in prison. Mr. and Mrs. Walter, the newspaper report said, did weep as the judge acceded to their wishes.

It is a small story of generosity and forgiveness, of a grieving man and woman responding to death by trying to give life instead of seeking vengeance. It is a story to stop us in our complaints, a powerful tale of contemporary redemption, a true story to remember.

CHAPTER 10

Thinking About Death

Elisabeth Kübler-Ross, the distinguished psychiatrist, has spoken many times about the phenomena that she considers proof of an afterlife. The evidence comes from the testimony of persons considered medically dead who, after being revived, report an experience of great peacefulness and a sensation of being suspended above the scene of their death. This current approach seems strangely separate from Dr. Kübler-Ross's previous work with the dying, which is rooted in the rich earth of human experience and struggle, with the tensing of every physical and psychic muscle in the face of advancing death; it is work keyed to a soaring but pure theme of ordinary existence, the battle that cannot be won but which is not lost, either, by the brave in their lunging and grappling with the angel of death—a tale of pain and howling, of anger flaring finally hot enough to make a forge for face-on wisdom and peace at the end.

Dr. Kübler-Ross joined herself to the struggle that so many others have looked away from, patiently translating for the rest of us the symbolic language spoken by those assaulted unexpectedly by death. A simple language when it was finally all known, a tongue for the shock of surprise and the longing for companionship in the dark hours, a tongue sharp enough for the curses of resentment and the final blessings of peace. Hers is a lasting contribution to our understanding of life rather than death, for it is life whose pulse she has helped us all to feel—the rhythmic signal of a dignified battle in progress between people stripped of every power but that of their own spirit—yes, a battle between them and quiet, surefooted death itself.

But this latest series of reports is extracted from another file, from the yellowed folders left by Conan Doyle and the other psychic searchers in the mists of ectoplasm; it is a turn away from the majesty of life pitted against death, a step back behind the curtains into the stale air of the séance. Science asks less and faith asks more of us when we whisper our intimations of immortality; science would take the simplest explanation for such phenomena and faith would look for something deeper, something that matches better the energies of life itself in the moments after death.

Death is a stubborn mystery and it does not give in easily; it is stronger than a floating dream, more ruthless in its demands and effects on us. A believer, even just a respecter of the awesomeness of death, must wonder at some of our contemporary efforts to tame death, to tranquilize ourselves in its presence as though it were not edged with dread in its every visitation. Better to stare at Gramp, the old coal miner photographed by his grandsons as he stumbled like Don Quixote across the scaly wastelands of his last struggle with death* Find here the wild blind eye of death, and smell too its fiery and destructive breath blackening the old man's last efforts at dignity. Death remains our savage visitor, familiar but ever strange, an enemy not to be embraced before we take his measure.

Death won't be processed and it cannot be pasteurized, although Americans have set themselves to these tasks. The

* *Gramp,* M. & D. Jury, 1978, Penguin.

American genius for establishing the principalities and the powers of industry, the laid-out charts of the Rotary and the Moose can be sniffed here. We not only want to deny death but we also want to organize dying itself, forcing it into orderly and comprehensible categories, making it something that can be dealt with as though it had no deep veins of mystery, no shafts of terror—and finally no meaning for thoroughly modern persons.

So the educational managers package death into high school courses in which students devise their own funerals, visit cemeteries, play, in a sense, with the surface of death and intimidate themselves and their own best instincts in the effort. The strangeness may disappear, but the mystery of death outwits such a curriculum. The gospel of contemporary eschatology does not stir the blood. Blessed are the resigned who go quietly and without a fight into the inescapable arms of death.

Such passivity, winking a friendly eye at us, waving an inviting hand our way, is not life at all. It is a subtle flavor in the narcotic that numbs us all into the state of junior executives, too terrified to do anything but gratefully accept the pink slips of our earthly dismissal. Believers are not given the trembling gift of life to surrender it without a fight; believers are not born to be edged off the planet and into the maw of eternity without ever laying claim to the power of life, without ever knowing what it is all about.

Enough of making death like a visit from a waxen mortician who lays a firm, pearl-gray gloved hand on our arm and leads us quietly away. If death is not more than that, then neither is life. If death does not ring with the power of a thousand bells, then eternity is full of silence too. It becomes a bland and unkept promise, a hint of our immortality no stronger than an ancient thought briefly recalled in some radiating mind of the cosmos. What can we pit the promises of faith against if death is all gentleness and sweet savorings? If death is not strong, then we cannot proclaim that love is stronger.

If death is an efficiency expert, quiet and lithe as a cat as he times our moves for the well-oiled running of the universe, then life is a promise bloated with air. Is not life itself, at every turn, still filled with every hint of dread, with multiplied signs of the mystery in which we are caught up together? Death demands more than a weary person's assent to the judge's sentence; it demands a fuller presence in life, the only place in which we find the half-clues about our passage to immortality.

Where indeed can we look? If not in the hoverings of ghosts over our deathbeds, then where? We invest our faith in life in the simple moments of which Dr. Kübler-Ross herself has written, in those times and experiences in and through which we achieve some deeper sense of ourselves and our possibilities, in an immersion in the turbulent waters of existence. For here abstract theology is made flesh and here we feel the tests of life just as we can feel the pull of death in all our days. We find testimony to eternity in the time we fully inhabit; yes, time, that strange flowing mystery, which demands, as death does, a struggle from us if we are to lay hold of its meaning.

That is why love cracks open the vault of time, challenging and finally conquering death itself. In the moments in which we say yes to love, we taste the clear water that springs up to life everlasting. We are fully alive when we love, carried out beyond our own boundaries on its tide of mystery until we can glimpse the very edge of existence and, for a fleeting instant, see beyond it as well. We are filled with life and find death in a thousand faces and guises, in the limits and endings, in the griefs and broken places of affection, in the yearning to close the gaps of separation that open up even for the truest of lovers.

We must let go of everything we possess if we are truly to grasp life's meaning; love breaks itself open over and over in order to grow into something more, in that space which lovers must finally leave between each other, in the freedom they must grant willingly to their children or their students, in the strange mystery, worked and reworked into our days, through which we love and die. Faith closes the gaps the way electricity leaps across the emptiness between two terminals; this is an experience filled with fire that lights up what lies across the darkened limits of our human experience.

Eternity floods the senses in those moments in which, in order to share life with others, we have to give some of our own away. We catch the tide and know that we are on course at those times in which we drink from the bittersweet springs of the suffering and death that mingle with the passionate flow of life.

CHAPTER 11

Do You Ever Feel Like Crying?

Tears say a lot but sometimes they are difficult to understand. We can weep for joy just as we weep for sorrow; some people weep at almost anything, while others hardly ever weep. Tears are a language that everybody speaks, but with different accents and meanings, according to the complicated laws of how we have learned to express our emotions. The French, they say, cry quite freely, while Americans shed private tears to express something very deep in their lives. How can something so wrenching to the soul be described as "having a good cry"?

The truth is, of course, that we have all felt like crying, and we know from experience that it can have many meanings. Tears can be the recourse of children who are on the spot—the defense against adult questioning or accusation that wins them mercy rather than justice in the small missteps of childhood. These are the tears that must be put away if a person is to move into maturity.

Sadly enough, there are those who go on weeping the defensive tears of childhood for the rest of their lives, whenever they are in difficult circumstances. These people never understand grown-up tears, the tears that are much more than the sobs of self-pity. Oh, we can all feel sorry for ourselves at times, but if we are relatively mature we can catch our emotions and save ourselves and others from the self-indulgent tears we might otherwise shed.

Tears in the mature person's life come at very deep moments of sadness and joy, on occasions of separation and reunion, whenever love shows through in life. Tears are above all a sign that we are alive, that the heart still beats because we care enough about someone or something to cry. Only the dead or the totally despairing have no tears. People who live with hope and trust can cry aloud; they are alive and have known the meaning of love.

Some men hide their tears to show their strength; others keep sorrow secret because weeping seems a source of shame for them; and heavyhearted are those whose eyes are dry because their wound is so deep that they cannot let the hurt out at all. The loneliest of men are those who have no one in whose presence they feel free to weep, no one whose responding love can redeem them from the sadness that has settled into their souls.

It is not an easy thing to cry, but neither is it a bad thing. It is a tragic thing to cry alone because this means we have built walls around our lives, walls so high that nobody else can see over them. Our tears not only express the deep wells of our feelings but they also make us one with all men who have ever loved or tried to reach out in a tender and caring way to anybody else. Our tears, Dickens said, are "rain upon the blinding dust of earth, overlying our hard hearts." Our tears redeem us when they reveal us clearly to another, unshielded from the consequences or risks that are involved in being human.

If we ourselves have cried, we find something of ourselves to give back to the suffering and sorrowful all around us. We need not move away from them, bidding them to hide their tears because they hurt us so much. We have gone along the same human path and we understand how, in our grief, the presence of another person can bring a certain wholeness to our sorrow. We give life when we learn from our own weeping how to give ourselves with gentleness and compassion to the sighs and struggles of other people. Mature tears are signs of the same kind of longing—a kinship with a world as yet unfulfilled. Our tears tell us that we are alive, that we have roots in the lives of others, and that we have been touched by the warmest of suns—human love. We should resolve that nobody we love ever has to cry alone.

CHAPTER 12

A Journal of Sorts

When you travel you are supposed to have the best of educational opportunities: a change of scene, interesting places and people, and no homework to do. Well, the last few months have been filled with travel for me and it has been an education, there is no doubt about that. . . . If you travel around America you will find goodness in the streets, and all you have to do is open yourself to it just a little and you will be enlarged by it. When you are with men and women trying to live honestly and simply, they literally inspire you to take the next steps forward just when you are almost overcome with weariness. Yes, the great mysteries are in the small moments, and they are all around us all the time.

Think, for example, of the genuinely thoughtful people around us. Oh, one understands that it is easier to identify the thoughtless members of our mixed-up human family, but there is a lesson about goodness even in this. Truly thoughtful persons never make us feel the pressure of the hand they reach out to us. That is why we don't notice them. Perhaps there is a better lesson about eternity here than in all the reports about the newly dead floating above themselves. For thoughtful people have a different relationship to time; it is not their master—indeed, their greatest strength lies in their capacity to break through the barriers of time itself and reach into the future, where they can accurately judge the way events will intersect. Their ability to do that—how much more exciting than the guessing game of seers like Jeanne Dixon!—is precisely what enables them to anticipate and to serve the needs of others so well.

They can read the future in matters as simple and as important as good manners, the possibilities of hurt feelings, and human needs as various as privacy or companionship, and then act to provide these for others. Thoughtful people are also good examples of the existential meaning of forgiveness. They give beforehand; they already understand our eccentricities or our failings and, with an acknowledgment if not outright approval of them, they make room for our flawed presence in life.

Maybe thoughtfulness is the molten core of whatever goodness exists at any level in our civilization. It is too simple, the searchers for mysticism say, to be the energy of sanctity, and, the superspiritual add, too natural—you know, not abstract enough, nor perhaps arcane enough, to suit them. And yet it is worth our contemplation. For thoughtfulness is purchased at a great price, at the high cost of our surrender of self-concern; it flows into existence only after the vessel of narcissism has been shattered. There is a plain, unmarked asceticism involved in thoughtfulness because it flourishes only in the lives of those who do not put themselves first; they have learned a secret filled with power: that the more we give up our own feelings, the freer we are to move lovingly in the lives of others.

And these thoughtful people are all around us. We don't notice them because they are so good at what they do and they do not send us invisible statements of psychological charges at the end of each month. Nor are they much concerned about proving their spirituality, a tendency that has become quite marked in many others of late. Who can doubt that a riptide of ascetic competition is breaking around us when we hear people arguing about whether or not they have been born again, and it is too bad that you have missed it. . . .

Well, thoughtful people seem to look at life more simply, and because of this they also can see more of it. That is another of their strengths. Just as they challenge time, so they also challenge space. Thoughtfulness transcends the limitations of both of these dimensions of life. It does not depend on physical presence or contact and its effects, since thoughtful people are freed of the constraints of time that accumulate and last in us. Thoughtfulness is something we can take with us long after the stage of other spiritual efforts has been struck.

Perhaps loving parents know more about thoughtfulness than anybody else. They cannot remain loving parents unless they do. But all the power of their love is expressed in a hundred ways, in the boundaries and the freedoms, in the limits and the faith they communicate to their children. It is no casual job; indeed, all the elements of what we finally recognize as important can be discovered in a cross section of loving parental life.

Good parents are still all around us, doing their best in a difficult and sometimes discouraging world. Add to their number the simple, direct thoughtfulness of those who remember our distress or needs from other directions—the old friends who write, the people who pray for us, the host who has taken the trouble to prepare our favorite meal, the stranger, even, who reaches out to us when we share a common predicament or challenge. No, it is not very exotic, this small virtue, not flashy enough to build a movement on, and yet it remains, from coast to coast, the best evidence I have seen of the action of goodness in our lives. . . .

One cannot deny that there are disconcerting experiences attached to travel in America. For one thing, it begins to seem that if you have been anywhere in the United States, you have been everywhere. Just drive down the main street of almost any town or suburb. Gradually, like invaders who dig in silently at night and whose billowing tents we only discover at dawn, the hamburger stands, the pizza huts, the fish-and-chip shops—each flying their own distinct banners with strange devices—have become the environment of our lives. One could cry out for the return of billboards after enough passages down these food-franchise thoroughfares. A song once spoke of a boulevard of broken dreams; actually, it is a boulevard of golden arches and chicken buckets—no broken dream but a kind of nightmare.

After a while you begin to think that ferrying between these establishments is life, that they are its only nourishers and symbols, and that there is no escape. Eating the same food in exactly the same setting—that is becoming the best metaphor for American life. The mystery of a meal—it is, after all, a sacred event, a place for friends, the sharing that makes us more than strangers—is obliterated by the very fact that it is never a mystery at all, that the mills will grind out their special burgers, fries, and shakes eternally and will give us all cancer or at least cavities in the end.

It may take a strong will and God knows what ingenuity to avoid living in the great plastic trough of fast eateries that line our avenues. They give a lie to the old phrase "You can't go home again."

With the fast-food chains all around, you can never really leave home. In fact, it might be wise to check the symptoms of McDonalditis, a common low-grade infection. When the people in the hamburger stand begin to look just like the people in the ads for the hamburger stand, then it may be time to change your life-style. When life begins to imitate art, the advertisers have conquered, and the search for fresh air and freedom must become our passion again. Or at least, my journal tells me, that's the way it seems all across America. . . .

If the chain restaurants don't get you, the music will. It is one of the other elements, along with the cloned motels, that mean that no matter how far you travel, you are not really getting to any place different. All the "comforts" of home are provided over and over again, like a looped tape, and not the least of these is furnished by the FM stations—not the rock ones, mind you, because that is another story—that play the sweetest music, in almost the same sequence, wherever you are in America: in your car, in the elevator, in the supermarket, yes, and the other day it was in my dentist's office. You could catch diabetes listening to this music that fills the atmosphere of America with sounds so sweet. The problem is that the sameness has a tragic kind of comfort to it. It lulls us with its familiarity, but it kills our souls at the same time. The mixture of sweet music, hamburgers, and CB chatter finally leaves our souls so stuffed with indigestibles that we suffer malnutrition of the spirit. There is no time for silence, nor room left for things of depth. There is no place where mystery can take root and grow in our lives. Every journey, like every meal, becomes the same, and we have no time to think or dream humanly. Perhaps we need to think about the problem and make sure that we save some room—as well as times and places—to rediscover what is unique about us and our lives.

CHAPTER 13

Uncounted Blessings

We are all well aware of our problems; hardly a day goes by that we do not think about them or that we are not reminded of them by others. Our troubles seem to multiply like rabbits, arrive like unexpected guests, and surrender their places only to other problems. We may also be aware of big blessings—or at least of the things that we classify that way—such as wealth or good looks. And we are properly grateful for the big gifts that the Spirit gives to us—love, good families, and health enough to enjoy them all.

What about the blessings that sometimes seem to be so hidden beneath our woes that we can hardly see them: These are the blessings we do not count so often, the small ones, as important as the bricks in a building's foundation, that support us even when we do not think about them. When we are feeling down or are tempted to dramatize ourselves as modern-day Jobs it is worthwhile to inspect the blessings that we can count on even if we do not count them up very often.

The word "blessing" may be used loosely in the modern world but it is not to be confused with any species of good luck. It is very different to call an experience a blessing rather than a lucky break. Blessings have nothing to do with luck charms, astrological charts, or vague benevolent wishes. Blessings are deeper, more lasting, and clearly related to our attitudes toward each other.

A blessing is a sign or a seal that notes that a transaction has occurred between persons that has changed both of them for the better. This could not, however, take place if the partners to the blessing were not ready to give away something of themselves. Blessings fall like spring rain when people are unselfish and trusting, standing in that special zone so close that they can feel each other's breath of concern. This is why blessings, even very modest ones, give us hints of what is sacred and eternal; they are lights from our shared fires that enable us to see beyond ourselves.

A blessing can generally be told by its effect on us. When we say that a person or an event has been a real blessing in our lives, we usually indicate that because of it we have been transformed, that we can see more inside and outside ourselves, that more of us is alive and involved with the things of life that have genuine meaning. A blessing, in other words, gives us a better sense of ourselves; it is nourishment and healing that strengthens us for our journeys. The person who brings a blessing can be recognized because he or she brings peace in the midst of conflict and comfort in the midst of sorrow. They do something for us without necessarily doing something to us.

Blessings make us feel friendlier and freer to live in and with a shadowed world that is still capable of betraying us. Blessings do not transport us to a Disneyland of virtue, a kingdom from which bad intentions have been banished. They do not make evil go away but they give us the light to focus on and do what is right for ourselves and others. Blessings differ from good luck charms because they deal with what is present in us, with flinty reality rather than ill-loved illusion.

Blessings may also be understood as graces that enable people to live. Blessings make sense as the kind stars of common life that enable us to live more humanly. It is, for example, a blessing to understand the uses of material things so that we can make them serve the larger purposes of human needs. Things become burdens when they are goals grown isolated in themselves; they wear us down when they no longer help people to understand more richly their own human significance. A blessing permits us to sense our inner needs and to give them the proper priority in life. There is no one as dissatisfied—perhaps we should say unblessed—as the person who has many possessions but who has not purchased inner peace and meaning.

Some of the blessings that are not always counted include the following:

That we can believe even though we have been sorely tried by our disappointments in others or with the partial disintegration of our own plans and dreams. It is an uncounted blessing to be able to go on believing, to continue to invest ourselves in other people even though we have the scars of many hurts. If we turn cynical, trading our blessings for curses, we face into what the poet A. E. Housman once described as "nothing but the night." To be able to believe means that we are still alive to the possibilities within ourselves and others; this means that we can face doubt and discouragement without caving in. Being able to believe holds life together for all of us.

That we have friends we can count on; that, as a matter of fact, we have friends that we have not even met yet. It is a blessing still to be able to be surprised by the mysteries of meetings and relationships which, even in very simple forms, still wait for us along the path of life. There is as much wonder in this as in most retreats. To retain the openness to make room for others in our lives enables us to look on life as something that is always just beginning. This is a blessing which says that, in a way, we can never grow old.

That we have seen or felt the silent and sometimes invisible experience of growth in our own lives and in the lives of others. To have observed growth gives us hope for the small miracles by which we are continually transformed or converted to a fuller realization of ourselves. The pace of growth is, however, difficult to observe or measure; sometimes we can only understand it as we look back and see the victories we have achieved, some of the maturity we have finally laid hold of. This perspective enables us to have hope for the future, to realize that as we have been blessed in the past, so we can count on the blessings of small steps of growth in the future.

That we have done the right thing even in difficult circumstances. This is also something that can best be seen afterward, the kind of experience through which we indeed become more of ourselves. We achieve a wholeness of personality that we can accomplish in no other way when we make difficult but right choices. It may be difficult to listen to the voice of conscience or to live by principles, especially when many other people seem to ridicule or ignore them, but if we do, no one can ever take this away from us. Thomas More once wrote of how sad it was that some people wore their wishbone where their backbone belonged. It is refreshing sometimes to look back over newspapers or magazines that are a year or two old. (Perhaps your dentist's office holds this surprising blessing.) In them you will see reflected some of the popular opinions of the day; many of these have not become unfashionable; others are totally rejected. The person who consistently tries to do the right thing moves through time unshaken by these fads because he or she operates out of a deep and consistent sense of the self. It is a blessing that begs to be counted.

That we have known grief which, although painful, is a testament to the fact that we have been close enough to others to make a difference. Sorrow only visits a loving heart, one that has been vulnerable enough to let somebody else share it. Nobody likes to grieve, although it is a necessary and inevitable human experience; it may be counted a blessing because it bears true witness that we have loved and been loved by others.

That we haven't got everything we want. Saint Theresa said that "more sorrow comes from answered prayers than unanswered prayers." We are, in fact, sometimes poor judges of what we need or should have, and half the time when we get what we think we want, we are not quite as content as we thought we would be. It is an uncounted blessing to come to terms with a life that does not automatically provide everything we want. The blessing lies in our resultant need to take account of the wants of others and of balancing our desires against theirs, of making room for them in our own lives. We are almost always enlarged when we do not get what we want, just as we are sometimes sadly diminished when we do.

The best blessings—the only real blessings—are those that are seeded with an awareness of life and its possibilities. Blessings are related to hope and promise, to belief in people and in what they can become. A blessing, then, is a commitment in faith to other persons which means that we hold them in a special kind of relationship, that our pledge to them is so sacred that wherever they go, so too do we.

We bless people when we give them something of ourselves that we will never ask them to give back. Some of the ways in which we do this are as follows:

By believing in them even to the extent of allowing them the freedom to make their own mistakes, to learn from their own experience something about the important truths of life. How difficult to trust other persons in this manner! And yet it is a taproot blessing for both them and us.

By standing by them, especially when they discover their mistakes and must harvest their regrets. This is when a person needs the encouragement of those who can still accept and stand by, no matter what the difficulty is. Standing by people does not mean standing in for them; it does not suggest we take over their problems or carry away their burdens. We bless them by joining our strength to theirs so that they can better do these things for themselves.

By leaving people alone. This seal on every blessing between people depends on knowing when not to interfere and when to keep our mouths shut. We can be very tempted to say to others, in effect, "I told you so," but this is the coldest of declarations when others are trying to straighten out their lives. Let them find the way that is right for them. To leave people alone does not mean to abandon them, but it means, in a real sense, to let them be. We thereby bless them with the gift of their own separateness, allowing them to have their own existence and yet to know that they can still call on us if and when they need us.

None of these blessings costs anything in terms of cash. They are blessings because they depend on the gift of ourselves, freely, truly, once and for all given.

CHAPTER 14

Longing

Every person knows the experience of longing. Men and women long for many things in a lifetime, and no matter what they acquire or achieve, the ache of longing is never completely eased. It is a sign of our continuing incompleteness; we cannot hold our most wondrous moments in focus for long; we cannot trap time nor stay change, the elements that eat away at every life; we move or are moved relentlessly forward, always searching but never quite finding enough to fill us.

In every age people have longed for other goals: wealth through alchemy, an earthly paradise through voyages of discovery, and, in our own time, contentment through affluence. We have only yearned more deeply as we have faced the disillusion of getting what we thought we wanted, or the disappointment of grasping at the mirages that dot the journey of life. It is never quite all there, and so we feel that we are never quite all there either.

The saddest part of our present plight is that we grasp at the shadows of superficial values in our quest for fulfillment. Our deepest longings, however, transcend the latest styles in clothes and automobiles. They reveal the emptiness of our current search for an erotic nirvana and the utter loneliness at the top that follows upon an aggressive hunt for power. These goals do not match our nature and so they multiply rather than relieve our longing.

Only real-life experience in seeking to love others responsibly brings each of us to an understanding of ourselves and the kinds of values for which we truly yearn, no matter how disguised our gropings may be. At the level of faith, hope, and love we know our greatest longing and can receive our most fulfilling response. It is also, of course, where we know our most painful disappointments. Believing, hoping, and loving bring us to life, but they also make us vulnerable in a way that we can never be if we shield ourselves from these experiences.

A husband, for example, can replace his marriage with his job. He protects himself from facing the demands of loving his wife and children by plunging into work, so that it keeps him at a defensive distance from them. So, too, a wife can find many distractions with her job or social calendar, but these leave the core of her life quite empty and unexplored. Any of us can do this in a culture that proposes so many pleasurable distractions that they prevent us from ever knowing who we are and keep us from testing ourselves in the trusting and loving that give life its meaning.

The worst danger of our present civilization is in the ease with which it provides escape from life, the way it can exempt us from facing the real issues of our identity as human beings. We have manufactured countless wonders and a thousand distractions that bring us no closer to understanding ourselves. Self-understanding follows a painful path, and there are progressively fewer who are willing to take it. The strange thing is the reverse paradox that is provided by this. The more we can have the goods of life, the less we are able to deal with the riches of our own personality and the more we are estranged from self-understanding. The more we want to avoid death out of fear, the less able we are to taste life. But longing, somewhere deep down where the sparks of our humanity are still fiery bright, will make us restless and we wonder why. Inoculated against the deepest feelings of our nature, we will long for them all the more. The cost of living is high, but the price of longing rises higher.

Longing remains a significant clue about us. It is not something to be smothered or disguised. It reveals the depths of our nature and points to the equally deep level of experience that constitutes the ground of life.

CHAPTER 15

A Retrospective

Are you as tired as I am of the summaries and surveys of movies and television, or of the retrospective tributes to various celebrities that have so often filled television screens? And one could be even more tired of the roasts and similar uncomfortable gatherings that have celebrated now this star and now that. Are you tired of the snippets and pieces, like baskets of fragments, that have been served up as our entertainment?

Perhaps as an antidote you can have your own retrospective, one that has the advantages of being more personal if not absolutely more entertaining. This does not require that you do much, although reviewing some of your records will prove quite stimulating. Look at your checkbook, for example, for its tales are more revealing than a detailed diary. One can be selective in diaries, but check stubs are as cold and uncompromising as wind from the top of the world. There, with dates and exact figures, we have a chronicle of our passage through the last year, an unchangeable record of what we thought worth buying, doing, or giving away, and in exact sequence. It reveals values, mistakes, perhaps a few regrets. One thing cannot be denied; it is a warm trail to follow if we want to learn more about ourselves.

Or look at your appointment calendar and think again about how it got filled and what guided your judgment, and what got done and what didn't. Let your mind explore the reality of all those days, counted out forever, that hold the story of your life. Were you too busy or not busy enough, or were you, in fact, not as busy as you made it look? The shape of our personalities can be found in these pages, the profile of our lives and their purpose. Where did we go and why? And what, now that the pages are all flipped over, did we accomplish? There may be more comfort than distress in such an inspection. It is worth doing anytime.

So, turn off the television recollections of scenes you may not remember very well anyway, and explore the retrospective evidence of your own life. One guarantee can be offered: You will learn far more about yourself than you will in almost any other activity.

CHAPTER 16

◆━━◆◆◆━━◆

Our Children Stopped Going to Church

The once serene universe has delivered a flurry of blows to the adjustment of adults during the last decade. And future shock stands like an obscure menace in the wings. One hardly needs to recount the seeming changes in values and behavior that have dizzied us so; former gangster Mickey Cohen proved an unlikely but accurate spokesman for many people when he said recently, "What's lacking in society today, I think, is nobody has any shame whatsoever, no respect whatsoever, and no pride. . . ."

The problem for many is that what they have believed in, made sacrifices for, and built their lives on has apparently been cast aside as casually as last year's fashions. Numb as disaster survivors being asked personal questions by brass-hearted reporters, they can only utter fragmented answers. Were we wrong all these years in taking God, authority, and traditional morality seriously? Who started the sexual revolution while we committed ourselves to marriage and fidelity? When did the age of the rip-off replace old-fashioned honesty? Were we deluded to think that duty was really important?

There are many aspects to this phenomenon. Some center on the needs of parents and others on the needs of their children. Many bewildered parents feel that it is their fault that things have turned out this way. Life has turned sour just when they expected that it might begin to be sweet, and they blame themselves for it. Guilt is an easy emotion to arouse in most of us for a simple reason: We make mistakes easily and regularly. We can, if we care to, always make a case against ourselves. When it comes to something as important as children, questions and doubts can be dislodged in our minds like nesting birds from an oak tree. But is it good to feel bad, or right to feel that we have been so wrong?

Feeling guilty is a way of handling the situation. If there is something out of line, we want to right the situation. Blaming ourselves may be easier to bear than the thought that we live in an accidental universe where nobody is responsible—and therefore nobody can be blamed—for anything. Punishing ourselves about what we may have failed to do in the past can, however, make us miss the more profound meaning of this experience in the present.

It may be that the discovery that the younger generation behaves differently toward traditional religion is just another aspect of the way life challenges us all the time. Life does not give us much time for catching our breath or regrouping our forces; life just keeps throwing invitations at us to hurl ourselves more generously into the fray all the time. We are wiser when we realize that the dreamy goal of a graceful and sun-drenched retirement is more a hopeful illusion than something we can count on. Besides, having no problems may not even be good for us.

It is better, in other words, to feel the pain of contradiction and uncertainty about those we love, better by far to continually examine the meaning of our relationships than to lean back and think that these things take care of themselves. The largest problem that many persons experience these days is boredom, a feeling of being on the outside of life and of needing distractions from its tedium in order to keep going. This is not true for people who love and care for others. They must constantly remain alive to each other or find that their love—and therefore most of the zest of life—dies by their own hand. The fact that adults care about their grown children means that they are never done with the basics of being human—never done with trusting and reaching out, and sticking with others even when they seem to move far away.

There may be some consolation in the fact that concern about the religious behavior of the younger generation can be something other than wailing, hand-wringing, and generally feeling bad about the situation. Good parents who gave generously of themselves while their children were growing now need to trust that what they did was fundamentally right, that the investment they made through loving sacrifice was a good one, and that it is far from lost or wasted. What good parents give to their children never disappears or evaporates or goes out of fashion; the loving elements that build another person are not perishable and, once given, they tend to last. When younger people seem to wander away from what we value as the symbols of our religious commitments, it is good to remember the many things we have done right rather than some of the ones that we have inevitably done wrong.

Just as parents one day come to trust their small children enough to let them explore on their own the limited world of their neighborhood, so they must keep on trusting them through adolescence and young adulthood while they explore other, larger, and more mysterious worlds. We believe that the lasting things given them by loving parents will stand them in good stead; that parents will provide the center of gravity and the guidance system that will enable young people to find their way home again.

What can adults do during these times when their children seem to be drifting on a long lead far away from them? They can attempt to understand and they can continue to live according to their own convictions. Youth seldom profits from the adults who try to transform themselves into young people again; and there has been a lot of that going around. They grow in relationship to adults who remain consistently themselves but who are still able to appreciate things from the viewpoint of others. This is part of the operational definition of loving others; it is the kind of thing we do for others when we give them freedom and respect at the same time. When the young can feel the freedom to question but know that their parents try to understand and always keep the lines of communication open, they are almost sure to make good decisions about their own values and goals.

At the far edge of trust is that circle of genuine freedom in which people may decide to do things or to adopt attitudes that we would never choose for ourselves. This is the most difficult part in all relationships, the place where we can be hurt deeply when those we love use the freedom we give them to move away from us. It is possible, after all, that some young people will seemingly move away from formal religion or into religious systems that are far different from any with which we are either familiar or comfortable.

What else can believers do but keep their hearts and arms open for those they love no matter what paths they choose or what decisions they make? That is what makes it different from the complicated bartering that is sometimes called love. The love of real believers is strong even when their hearts are sore from the hurts that can batter them in the close range of family life. The gift we make of ourselves to those we love is not conditioned on their believing, praying, or pleasing us in any way. The aching and abiding challenge of life is to accept and love others for their sake and never to turn into misers with our affection or stingy accountants of our compassion. Error, they used to say, has no rights. Yes, that is true; but those who err still have their human rights.

Even if things don't work out quite the way we would like, we lose nothing in being openhearted and generous in our attitude. This is the kind of attitude that clearly tells people what we believe in and what we value. It is always worth trying to do with as much sincerity as we can muster. It means that we make of ourselves a true home, a place people can always come back to, a place, as Robert Frost once wrote, "where, when you have to go there, they have to take you in."

CHAPTER 17

How Do I Treat Myself?

This is a good question because its answer tells us more about ourselves—and may lead us to treat ourselves more sensibly and more humanly—and it also assists us in understanding our relationships with other persons. For our attitudes toward our own selves and toward others are interwoven strands of the same psychological reality and the one reflects the other. If we become more sensitive to what we are actually like, the chances are we will become the same to others. Everything gets better when we approach our own personalities with greater understanding. We give the best parts of ourselves a break and we more easily forgive the aspects of ourselves that are immature, mystifying, or, at times at least, apparently just plain crazy.

Well, how do we treat ourselves? What is the transaction like? Does it resemble writing a letter or is it more like sending a bill? It may be more like passing a law or, on occasion, sentencing a prisoner. Sometimes we regard ourselves with unflagging suspicion, as though we were tower guards surveying ourselves in the yard below. None of these arrangements are very comfortable, of course, because they all reflect a certain hesitancy about ourselves and our poorer possibilities.

There are some people, of course, who do not regard themselves suspiciously but expectantly; they are always half-filled with longing for approval from somewhere out-side of themselves—from teachers, parents, or employers—and dark are their moods when this praise is not forthcoming. Still others have different and more melancholy expectations; they live with themselves like somebody who is constantly under a tornado warning. The worst may happen at any moment, and so they survive, after a fashion, by holding their breath and waiting for the blows to fall.

One could devise longer lists, but these may prove sufficient to inspire a gentler look at ourselves and a willingness to treat ourselves a little more fairly. This does not mean, obviously, that we let everything go or that we abandon discipline altogether. It suggests rather that a deeper and more understanding view of ourselves may lead to more real growth and personal development than all the harsh and anxious indictments that we may make of ourselves. Being more compassionate toward ourselves prompts us to design our goals more realistically and boosts our chances of accomplishing them.

Renewing ourselves does not demand that we remake ourselves entirely but rather that, like the earth itself, we draw on the life that is already present, the possibilities that have survived and that we give these a chance to grow.

CHAPTER 18

———————◆———————

Lasting Love

Most people, it seems to me, do much better with understanding than with condemnation. The prophets of doom like to talk about future shock, about the hazards of life in the next century, but the ordinary person has challenge enough just getting through the day at hand. This is not to say that life is totally oppressive but it is to recognize that it never lets up, no matter how old or securely retired people may get.

Life is like a package whose wrappings begin to loosen and uncurl as soon as we put the stamps on it. There seems to be some force of its own at work that uncoils at its own carefully planned rate to break through the best of our plans and to stir us to renewed action just when we thought we could take it easy for a while.

Perhaps the greatest wisdom resides in recognizing the mildly perverse quality of existence and the abiding validity of Murphy's Law that whatever can go wrong will do just that. If we can anticipate life as a continuing journey over roads that are sometimes in bad repair, we will make the trip far more successfully. If we are prepared for things to get worse, we are able to make them better by that very insight.

So, as a corollary, we should try to eliminate the unnecessary suffering in our existence because there will be plenty of necessary suffering anyway. No need, then, for the average man and woman to seek extraordinary hardships, or to foster unrealistic expectations about life, for these merely lead to suffering that we do not need and that we can do without quite nicely. There are enough tests in handling the challenges that our spirits sustain on almost any day of the week in doing our work, loving our friends, and deepening our family ties.

The thing about life that so many persons do not suspect is that it gives us something only if we are always giving something of ourselves first. Many persons expect love to come along, like some romantic traveler, and take care of them. But, mysterious as it may seem, love does not take care of us unless we are ready to take care of each other. Love grows only as we give and, in the deepest of relationships, there is no end to giving.

So, love is indeed a puzzle, because while it is a gift it is also a summons, and it usually comes to us when we are looking the other way. Lasting love comes to those individuals who are not seeking it self-consciously but to those who have broken out of their own concerns and who have forgotten themselves. That is why it seems a surprise and an unexpected blessing; it fills the hollows of our hearts that we have made empty through generosity to others.

Lovers know well the challenge presented by life's loose ends. As a matter of fact, only persons with a fairly well established identity can truly love each other very deeply and over a long time. What lovers recognize is that, howsoever deep, the love they share is always incomplete. Indeed, this incompleteness is a characteristic of real love. It tells us that love does not stay the same and that it does not move backward. Love changes as it moves steadily into the future, now angling to the side a bit and now reaching out almost beyond the limits of endurance in order to keep up with our human experience.

Love, however, always reaches beyond and never closes itself finally on one event or one situation. A condition of staying in love is that we live with the truth that love cannot be fixed in time; it is not the kind of precious possession that can be displayed in an airless glass case so that we can admire it at a particular moment of fullness. Love never reaches fullness; it is always reaching toward it. If it is not loose-ended, it is open-ended. Whenever we try to have it in any other form, we begin to kill it.

Sometimes these events or happenings turn out to be the most upsetting or dismaying of life's loose ends. These are the things that we don't really fit into what we know of ourselves and of life—unexpected occurrences that are out of phase with the rhythm of our lives which therefore we experience as alienating. In experiencing them we seem like strangers to ourselves and to the world with which we have been familiar. It is difficult to integrate these events into our sense of self. We seem sticky-fingered at getting the combination or at finding the key to unlock their meaning in a satisfactory manner. These are loose ends that just hang there because we cannot find the right symbol or the right word that makes sense for us. They include:

A sudden, unexpected stress or an intimation of dread creeps in its unexplained way into our life space. It is part of the mystery of evil, the perennial impossibility of dealing with the loose ends that are inevitably a part of the suffering of the innocent, the untimely death of the young, or the injustice sometimes meted out to the meek and humble of heart. Although these things have occurred before, there is something perennially challenging about them. They do not seem to make sense, and as long as they do not touch our immediate lives, we feel no urgency to think or even pray about them. So we are always struggling with the problem of evil, not as a remote and abstract possibility but as a reality which we are tempted to think has a life of its own. It is difficult to come to terms with evil because it is hard to give a name to such a deceitful force, and harder still to locate and accept our own capacity to hurt others or forget what we should remember or fall short of our ideals.

There is a loose end in the sudden-change reaction on the part of someone we thought we knew well. This is literally an estranging experience because it seems to crack open the secure base of our relationship. How and why can this happen? It is so startling that sometimes we would rather just forget it and so not have to deal with understanding and labeling it correctly in our experience. We would rather forget than try to understand the other person and the way this reaction may fit into his or her own life.

A counterpart to this is our own sudden, seemingly new and inconsistent, behavior. Loose ends abound when we suddenly step out of character through giving in to a long-repressed impulse; when we suddenly release the controls that were far tighter than we allowed even ourselves to know. What was stirring in us all this while? What was it, we ask ourselves, that we had never acknowledged but which abruptly broke the image of our polished self-containment? We say, "That's not like me," or "I've never done anything like that before." But the behavior did not come out of midair. It came out of ourselves and it has roots that we can trace if we take the time and have the patience and understanding toward ourselves that is necessary for uncovering the important meaning of such events.

There is the uneasiness, the stalking restlessness that cannot be overcome, no matter how many guarantees of security we may pile up. It is a vague kind of anxiety, a kind of existential trembling that we cannot run away from. It arises when things do not completely fit together deep inside us. These may be hairline cracks in our psyche, but the anxiety seeps through and bids us to look once again at the unfinished business of our own maturity.

There is a homely but comforting law of life that tells us that we never do the really important things in life perfectly. It is only the unimportant things that we can master to a static kind of perfection—like learning a card trick, memorizing lines written by someone else, or polishing with practice a golf swing. We never achieve the same ease with the big and vital things like loving people or forgiving one another.

The reason is that the circumstances are always different and that each occasion demands something fresh and unrehearsed in our response. We cannot do these important things unless we are real—and, of course, we cannot be real unless we are also spontaneous and imperfect. That is the way it is in keeping in touch with those we love even when they move into worlds very different from ours. We love them in the only way we can—in that glorious, unfinished way that true love always expresses itself.

We shouldn't be surprised by this fact but rather encouraged because we are heading in the right direction. Keeping our hearts open is an ongoing process that we get better at but never get down perfectly. This is why genuine love works—it bridges the gaps in the human condition only when it comes from generous but flawed hearts.

CHAPTER 19

Who Is Beautiful?

You don't seem to hear quite so much about the "beautiful people" anymore. They are as out-of-date as the revolutionary students of the sixties. In the first place, calling them "beautiful" was probably a mistake, another example of how to misuse and thereby distort a perfectly good word. When party-going by bored people becomes our idea of beauty, we are badly estranged from a sense of ourselves as well as the meaning of life. So many of the beautiful people seem, even in recollection, to be unhappy, ardent pursuers of something they have had enormous difficulty in finding. One is reminded of the answer given by the rich lady when she was asked what went on in the fabled mansions of Newport during its heyday. "Nothing," she said, "nothing but gaiety and grief." What indeed is beautiful? What does it mean to us when we read . . .

In Canada one recent summer a forty-five-year-old man accidentally stepped in front of a passenger train. As reported in the *Toronto Star*, it wasn't suicide. The man in question had been left by a childhood disease with a disfigured face, which made him feel that he was the ugliest man alive. Because of this he always walked with his head down; his ugliness deprived him of the normal experiences available to other persons. He was rejected for the service because of his looks and never married. What social life he had was with a group of war veterans in the Royal Canadian Legion Clubhouse near his basement apartment.

There were tears in the eyes of the legionnaires, however, when they heard the news of the man's death. "He was a very ugly man, all right, but also one of the best guys I ever knew," said one of the men of the club, who had known him for fifteen years. "He had hundreds of huge welts on his face. He had real thick glasses and was a little guy. Children who saw him on the street were actually afraid of him. But the few children who got to know him loved him dearly." Another member said, "He was well liked and accepted by the 560 members here, and this is the only place where I think he really forgot about his looks. The guy really never got a break in life . . . he avoided people because he thought he revolted them, but he was actually a beautiful man when you got to know him." One of the executives of the legion proposed that the bylaws be relaxed to allow the Canadian flag to be draped on the man's casket. "The members want to go before his casket, salute, place their poppy on the flag and salute again, as they do in an official memorial service. We went through the hell of war, but he went through the hell of a lonely life, which is a much tougher battle. He was one of us. . . ."

Just a few weeks ago I sat across an airplane aisle from an extremely attractive woman in her early thirties. She seemed very conscious of her good looks, inspecting them frequently, and touching them up like an obsessive artist who could never finish a painting. It was only when she spoke that her appearance changed. Her voice was loud and shrill and it cut through the motor's roar as easily as an aircraft carrier slices through a wave. "I hate that person, I hate that person," she kept saying, "she's just a no-good piece of trash and I want nothing to do with her. . . ." Her tones made you feel that what she saw in her compact mirror was about all she could see in life,—herself. She seemed as ugly as her words.

Which of these two was beautiful and which was ugly? The answer is not hard to find. The story of the ugly man, his head down as he left the warmth of the legion hall, keeps us from feeling sorry for ourselves when we think that the world has treated us poorly. But both he and the unhappy woman also make us pause to reflect on what we see as beautiful around us. What do we look for? And what do we see?

The focus of our perceptions tells us a lot about ourselves. It informs us of the angle that we take in looking at the world or other people around us. It also indicates those things or events we selected out of our surroundings as of interest or concern to us. What do we focus on, in other words, and what does this tell us about ourselves? It not only says something about our notions of beauty but it also tells us something about our values and about the things we strive for. Beauty may be in the eye of the beholder, but self-knowledge springs back at us from the things that we behold.

It is easy, for example, to be taken up with the appearance of things. There is almost a national vulnerability to this difficulty, especially when we are defined as "in" or "out," depending on what we wear or whether we echo a popular opinion about things. We can strive, in other words, to be part of the picture, to fit into it so that we do not stand out as individuals. In this situation our aim is the social approval of others, the feeling of being up-to-date, in the swing of things, or whatever else it may be called at the moment. It is due to change in a few months anyway, and all those clothes, shoes, and attitudes may have to be recycled. The concern is for the surface, not the substance. It is an easy trap and a sad betrayal of even the possibility of understanding beauty or discovering our true selves; we settle for short psychological rations in these circumstances.

The difficulty is heightened when the world of advertising tells us that we can reach the cherished goals of life without strain, suffering, or even the need for gray hair. When the world has left you out—when you are an ugly duckling—redemption comes through changing your brand of soap, deodorant, or toothpaste. The secret of life lies in your medicine cabinet. Drink it, swig it, or apply it and you will be irresistible, the center of others' attention, and true love will be yours at last. It involves no work, no investment of time, none of the suffering that comes in the ordinary process of edging closer to one another. Nothing hurts, because in this view of things, nothing is felt deeply enough to be an occasion of pain. This despoils our sense of ourselves.

Bertrand Russell fancied the beauty of mathematics which he described as "a beauty cold and austere, like that of sculpture." There is something awesome about mathematical terms, those emotionless arcs that inhabit the cool world of graphs. The problem is that this kind of beauty is not found in the human situation. Persons need warmth and closeness to each other, conditions that are guaranteed always to be jumbled and colorful and imperfect. There is nothing wrong in this. In fact, there is everything right about it. As Francis Bacon once observed, "There is no excellent beauty that hath not some strangeness in the proportion." The realization that human beauty is never as flawless as geometric planes enables us to understand how the ugly man in Canada could be beautiful and the beautiful woman on the airplane could be ugly. Our sense of what is beautiful does not arise from using an art director's airbrush to retouch the blemishes of the human condition; it arises rather from our capacity to see people whole.

Beauty arises from the fullness of a person. It never depends on what someone looks like on the surface. We do not even see others well when we look from only one angle —say the sensual, for example—and then presume that we have seen everything about them. We need an eye for what one writer once called "the dim beauty at the heart of things." Real beauty is not skin-deep at all. It flowers from deep within, fusing the various levels of personality into a penetrating and lasting attractiveness.

Like any great art, a vision of what is authentically beautiful includes its flaws. It does not try to hide but it does try to understand them. Only individuals who are acquainted with their own capacity for evil can achieve the wholeness that makes them truly beautiful. Handsome persons are not naive; they have preserved a sense of reality and this enables them to face life straight on. They are not about to betray their sense of themselves nor of the meaning of life through any misplaced innocence.

Truly beautiful persons are also acquainted with humor and pain. These things show up on their faces regularly because they do respond to the basics rather than the accidentals in life. They have a wonderful transparency; they are alive and do not try to fake it. They do not choose the coolness of Russell's mathematics as a substitute for the less well-charted ways of ordinary living. It is the wholeness of their personalities which makes them beautiful; that is what we sense when we meet them. We say, "He is not really good-looking" or "She's not really what you'd call an attractive person" . . . followed by "but he (she) is really beautiful," Why? Because they are fully alive.

"There is too much beauty on this earth for a lonely man to bear," so the poet told us, and each of us must discover this truth for ourselves. It tells us some things about beauty and how we view and strive to attain it.

The beauty everywhere around us cries out to be shared, to be looked at with someone else. Perhaps the world only becomes truly beautiful when we no longer look at it only through our own eyes. The first step away from loneliness and isolation depends on breaking free of our own concerns and moving out of an overfocus on ourselves. There is something bittersweet in the realization of how much sharing in good but simple things enables us to appreciate their beauty. We remember moments when we looked on things with those we loved and so were enabled to recognize their beauty in a deeper way. The loneliness after sharing is painful but it has an awesome beauty about it. It is only present in the lives of those who have loved and who now miss but clearly remember what they have shared and meant to each other.

There is a spark in the experience of sharing beautiful things with someone else that enables us to see deeply into our own identity, into our need for each other, and into the redemption that comes to those who recognize the simple things as the important things in life. It makes it possible for us to reclaim the word "beauty" from those who cheapen it by misapplying it in shallow situations that do not deserve it. This occurs as we return to the truth that it is love which makes people beautiful, that it is love which unlocks all of us and brings us to life.

CHAPTER 20

Hope Is Always with Us

It is certainly commendable to emphasize the positive sides of our personalities, the brave dreams and great plans about what we can become and what we can accomplish. Hope holds us together and it is the best of virtues to remember. Of course, we are all familiar with the optimistic cheerleaders of the human potential movement who, possessing everything but a tragic sense about life, raise visions of humanity remade through a variety of egalitarian creative exercises. Perfection for the masses is already a big business but it is finally a poor relation of hope, that ancient virtue filled with wrinkles and wisdom through which we come to terms with a not quite finished universe.

Hope is the very thing for humans who may not be able to respond to the beating drums and glorious parade drills of the human potential advocates. It is a state of mind, an attitude of the person, that enables us to live with our shortcomings and failures as well as with our possibilities and achievements. It is power for the soul for hard times and difficult tasks, for making our way through the narrow passages of illness and discouragement, a virtue to sustain all of us for whom so many things do not work out quite as we had hoped or wished. It is a gloriously human virtue that challenges darkness and separation and death; it is a simple virtue, durable for the long haul, and found in the most modest of our gestures and activities. Hope is not the stuff of grandiose promises nor of naive miscalculation and overconfidence; it resides in every reaching out to others, as much as to the crying and lost child as to the bereaved or anxious adult.

Hope is a virtue for every season and every trial of our existence, the one source of energy and purpose that is strong enough for the way life really is. It is the virtue for those who know that we cannot live on impossible dreams and who understand that it is through hoping we can touch and bring to life those possibilities that best define us.

You have surely read of novelist Saul Bellow's acceptance speech as a Nobel laureate. It is filled with signals of hope, with intuitions that, despite our problems, there is an abiding and unsatisfied core to human beings. He challenges contemporary writers with a question of what they would do "if they were to recognize that an immense desire had arisen for a return from the periphery, for what was simple and true?"

Saying that he is not sure what currently engages the energies of man, Bellow observes that life has created a yearning for what is more basic, "an immense, painful longing for a broader, more flexible, fuller, more coherent, more comprehensive account of what we human beings are, who we are and what life is for."

It is probably a good thing to consider our potential for odd experiences, especially at the start of a year which, for all we know, may be filled with them. Maybe the wisest axiom of life is that anybody is capable of doing almost anything. This does not mean that we might all steal or commit murder, but it does suggest that, given the proper circumstances, we might do a number of things that would surprise us or at least seem inconsistent for us. Just think of the times you have described yourself this way: "Well, it was a most unusual thing for me to do," or "You know I never do anything like that," or "It was the first time I ever felt that way," or some other variant of this theme. The fact is that, in minor ways, at least, we are always surprising ourselves and providing firsthand evidence of our own uniqueness.

It is a good thing, for example, to face and acknowledge our possibilities for evil. It is better to locate these in ourselves, even in our unexplained or seemingly remote selves, than to imagine that some force invades us and uses us for sinister purposes. We may not like to gaze on our capacity to hurt or to be indifferent or just insensitive; we may not wish to inspect our instinct for small acts of revenge or for making other people feel guilty, or for the indulgence of a dozen other hostile vanities, but those possibilities are there in each of us.

Then there is a whole category of reactions that are not evil but that are certainly surprising and which, for many people, are profoundly disturbing. This includes the areas of thoughts and feelings as well as the fantasies that can fly as eerily as bats through the caverns of our imagination. People obsessed with unwanted dreams think that they are signatories to a Faustian pact through which greater knowledge of evil is delivered to them because they have bartered away their souls; they do not savor their fantasies and they are horrified by some of their impulses. Where could these have come from? And the answer is that they come from inside, from the folds and crevices of the unconscious, from events no longer remembered, from the psychological stuff of our life histories, from the very fact that we are so thoroughly human. There is no shame in that.

It's in the unconscious that our possibilities for odd and

inconsistent behavior have their most snarled and meaty roots. We all possess the possibilities for occasional craziness, at least on a small scale, and we should learn to live with these slips of personality rather than just get mad at ourselves or vexed at what is so difficult to explain about ourselves. We are mysteries still, despite the maps of our genetic endowments that can now be drawn, and in the face of the numbers—from IQ to credit-card digits—that can be tallied about us. And one of our mysteries lies in our possibility for quirkiness, unexpected feelings, surprising fantasies, and inconsistent behavior.

But all this is not without hope for us. First of all, we would be devoid of charm if we were entirely predictable or if some cartographer could draw a satisfactory rendering of our personalities. What makes us interesting is our capacity for being different, even to ourselves. And it is another aspect of that same fundamental treasure that allows us to be more noble and more loving than we thought we could be; it is something impenetrable in our endowments that is the spark of our creativity, the soul of our best moments, the power behind the investments of faith and hope that we can make in others and honor through good times and bad. Our heroism arises from our uniqueness, from secret stores of strength that belong only to us.

Hope is the power through which we make our passage across the numerous broken places of life—can you count them all in any day?—across misunderstandings and hurts, to the far reaches of the love that stabilizes and gives meaning to all the minor moments that would otherwise be swallowed in the maw of time. It is hard to hope and to mean it because it does not come into existence through proclamation; it rises from our own response to living. It flows from the small-scale gestures of reaching out; yes, it lives in every one of them, from the helping hand to the loving embrace. It lives in all the small details we can hardly remember but which finally contain the meaning of our lives, which tell us what we mean to each other.

CHAPTER 21

The Mourning of Youth

Something strange has happened but nobody is quite sure what it is. One of the symptoms seems to be a sudden weariness with youth on the part of older people, as though a line, like an unmarked meridian in the ocean, had been passed almost without notice but not without consequences. Middle-aged people, the "command generation," as *Time* once called them, are tired of young people, which is to say that in some way their children have worn them out, excavated the last mine producing steady concern, and stand now not as enemies but as young adults who must, after decades of attention and adulation, after years at the very center of the American universe, step out on their own into the real world.

The older generation is not weary of youth as individuals but rather as a focus of constant attention, the way a slightly deaf person grows finally tired of straining to hear the softly slurred words of an inconsiderate visitor. It is as though older persons, expressing their love in a way that is new to them and certainly novel for youth, are shifting from an attitude of care to one of expectation. But the whole experience is bewildering to young people who have grown accustomed to a place near the center of gravity in their family life and who cannot quite understand nor accustom themselves to being anywhere else.

Young people have, in other words, suffered a loss, but it is hard to define and they are not sure how to mourn it. They feel depressed and out of place and unsure of whether or where they want to step next in a world that has suddenly become resistant or indifferent where it once danced in cap and bells for them. It is impossible to deny that the young people of today received a great deal of attention growing up. And it is impossible to deny that it was a difficult time in which to grow up.

Yet something has shifted and, raised without their learning much about the need for or the experience of delaying gratification, they cannot deal easily with an unresponsive environment nor a world that no longer defines them for themselves. Gone even is the military draft and they are robbed of a huge symbolic institution against which they were formerly able to perceive themselves. And the world is a mass of truculent strangers, unmoved by their plight, not altogether friendly and closing in on them like ancestors ready to press all the overdue bills of history into their hands.

Young people have lost something, the thing we all surrender sooner or later—a magical world in which we are omnipotent before we are suddenly crowded into the hard-edged alleys of maturity. Young people have lost something they would have had to give up sooner or later, but they have not been helped to understand the dimensions of the loss. It is small wonder that they hesitate at the edges of adult life, unsure of what they want to do, or of what they want to be, or of the process by which they will achieve the goals that are not very clear for them. Their loss is real and we should expect the searching symbolic activity of a period of grief for their lost magical years, for the time out of time that is no more, before they can integrate themselves into the forgiving world which seems such an alien place to them.

CHAPTER 22

————◆————

Waiting for Spring

We always wait for spring on guard against the tricks of a dying winter that is not above the entrapping sham of warm days before the calendar is ready for them—days that fool the youngest of buds and the oldest of hearts at the same time. False springs are the last weapon of the old warrior winter. But even the counterfeit days of a new season are welcome. We have waited long enough; let the spring come!

But what lessons of readiness and of the almost cruel discipline of waiting can we still learn from the visitation—like that of a hard-hearted landlord—of winter? They concern the abiding truths, the ones we learn and discover that we must relearn every year. There may be nothing more difficult for us to acquire than patience, that virtue so long out of sight that it seems out of mind as well.

And yet patience remains the grace through which we become possessors of our lives. For, like it or not, spring makes us wail against our every longing cry and prayer. We cannot force its full arrival any more than we can close our hands on it in the deceptive warmth of late winter days.

Spring comes in its own time and it will have its way with us. It is the season of hope and expectation. It is the interlude for hard lessons, for self-denial not for its own sake but in order to match our spirits to the rhythm of the

changing year, to help us grasp that the price of hope ful-
filled in spring is still our readiness to face the deaths, multiplied almost mercilessly, in the winters of our lives.

Perhaps it is the lesson of readiness that is hardest of all.
We live in a culture in which readiness of any kind seems
an idea from a past that is as dead, buried and forgotten as
the last casualty at Gettysburg. Readiness—that internal
maturity that depends on some mysterious combination of
growth and experience—is out of style when plants can be
made to bloom out of season and animals to fatten rapidly
through various scientific interventions. What need of
readiness when rock stars are made celebrities before they
learn how to sing and premarital sex is thought by so many
to be the rule rather than the exception?

Waiting for the moment of readiness seems archaic indeed when the demands of impulse and instinct are never
to be denied. And yet what is the result when people grab
for love or even friendship before they are strong enough to
bear their burdens as well as celebrate their joys? Has more
pain been delivered to the world through the discipline of
waiting or through the unwillingness to accept it as a solemn and mysterious fact of life?

If waiting is really a virtue called patience that we have
purposely avoided for a long time, self-denial is a closely
related virtue—and therefore just as ancient—that also demands our inspection. And it is being given increased public attention. For, having exhausted the possibilities of self-
indulgence, many persons are staggering toward renuncia-
tion as a feature of their life-style because nothing else has
worked very well. Having everything without delay, taking
such pleasures as are available the way children attack an
open box of chocolates—all this has not delivered happi-

ness, and sometimes it has not even provided much fun or pleasure either.

Getting along on less is a theme for a country struggling with an energy crisis, but it is the echo of the ascetic wisdom that has been part of every religious heritage. We are coming home the hard way because we cannot seem to get to nirvana by the route we had been taking. It is a return to familiar things, to the joys that lie on the other side of loving sacrifice, to the sense of personal integrity that arises from self-possession, to the deep peace that fills the lives of those who, unafraid to die, find a fullness of life.

CHAPTER 23

—◆—

The Challenge of Being Trusted

Trust has always been a favorite subject. Seldom has it been so much in vogue as now, when so many people are talking about the nature of public trust. The subject of personal trust has, of course, been much discussed because it strikes close to the heart of everyone's life. Even if you talk about trust funds, credit, or other related subjects, you cannot escape the common element of faith that runs through them all. Fidelity is intimately involved with any concept of trusting or being trusted. It is possible—indeed it happens regularly—to talk about trust and not understand fidelity. If, however, you have some appreciation for faithfulness, you will automatically appreciate the meaning of trust as well. It is as vital to our human and spiritual survival as air; and yet how hard it is to find air in a free and pure state.

We have a tendency to speak of trust as something bestowed, something we very much want from other persons. Whether you are a parent or a teacher, you can hear ringing in your ears, "Don't you trust me?" Trust is in itself a delicate thing, finely engraved with our most ancient longings and yet light enough to wear on the heart. But trust can also be used as a weapon, an instrument of interpersonal negotiation and demand. Emphasis can almost exclusively be placed on getting trust out of someone else.

We have often explored the terrors of placing our trust in others. There may be no more difficult commitment in our experience than that of surrendering our defenses in order to give our trust to other persons. But what does it mean to be on the receiving end of trust, to be the one to whom the commitment is made? Is the obligation, the investment, solely that made by the one who trusts? Is that where all the fabled "risk" of loving and trusting resides? Or is there an equally demanding and profoundly significant if unexpected role for those who are trusted?

There isn't any credit bank that exists in which one can look up the "humanity rating" of another person. Data files may tell how people manage their finances, but there is no repository of data about the way people manage their hearts. Shakespeare, in *The Merchant of Venice*, gave a partial answer to this question of trust: "The man that hath no music in himself, nor does not move with concord of sweet sounds: let no such man be trusted."

But what does it mean to have music in ourselves? Shakespeare is writing about the quality of responsiveness to life that is a basic signal of our involvement in existence and of our capacity to hear and understand what is going on in our particular share of it. It has to do with whether we are able to feel life and whether we understand that what we do reverberates in the lives of those around us. Being trusted means that we can receive the messages and appreciate their meaning, that we work at understanding and translating the significance of our lives, that we have passed out of the world of storybook relationships into a harder but richer awareness of others. Being trusted means that we can react to these important others around us and that we can change and grow in responding to them. Being trusted means we are ready to continue growing.

There is nothing that dies faster than love or friendship that people try to fix at a certain stage or at a certain time in their lives. Wanting their friendships never to change and trying to make them timeless, these people kill them. Friendship and love that are kindled by genuine trust, however, break through the bonds of time and give us a bright, if brief, intuition about eternity. When we are trusted we do not live in an enchanted forest but in the real world.

Being trusted means that we cannot be selfish anymore. What an old-fashioned idea! As receivers of trust we rediscover that we cannot live only for our own interests or think that we can hold our own time and space safe from everyone else. Being trusted involves us in the oldest and most inescapable of human processes, that of receiving the fullness of another person, which can only be acknowledged by our own willingness to surrender the fullness of ourselves in return.

There is a death involved in being trusted, a death to narrow views, stifling self-interest, and the illusion that we win something that we can use in any way we wish by demanding that others trust us. If we do not commit ourselves to our best effort, we destroy the exchange that is the essence of trust and scatter its riches like irretrievable coins into the sea. Being trusted is essential for the beginning of our lives; it is a basic exchange between parents and children. So also is it necessary for the continuation of our lives, but that does not liken trust to artificial respiration. Trust is another's breath given to us so that we might begin to breathe fully for ourselves. It is the life of another person offered freely so that we might discover and inhabit our own more fully. Being trusted is not just being left alone to do what we feel like. This kills trust because the one who so receives it is dead to its meaning from the very beginning.

At a time when people wonder whether there is anything about which to feel guilty, the violation of trust offers us clear ground for experiencing that emotion ourselves. The trouble is that, if failing in trust dulls our hearts, we may gradually become unresponsive to the world we create around us. Failing in trust is, however, something to feel guilty about. Many social observers over the last generation have commented about our lowering moral standards. Writers such as Erich Fromm and David Riesman have spoken about modern people relying on "other-directedness" rather than "inner-directedness" for the regulation of their behavior. When we are other-directed we attempt to avoid the experience of shame. Persons, great and small, can operate this way, seeing as the main deterrent to their activity the threat of being caught, punished, and therefore humiliated in front of others. They react to shame because they cannot feel guilty.

Inner-directed persons, however, have not lost their capacity to experience guilt and have not abandoned an inner view of themselves through which they judge the quality and meaning of their actions. Shame is something we get rid of when we say, "No one will ever know about this." That, however, does not handle the kind of guilt we should experience when we make a sacrilege of the trust invested in us by others. Failing in our acceptance of trust is worth feeling guilty about.

Sometimes we can break faith by making ruin of the trust that is given to us by somebody else. The other person, we sometimes say to ourselves, may never even know about it. Then, we are reassured by so many people in the modern world, because nobody else knows about it, they can't be hurt by our breaking of trust. This is exactly what is not true as far as trust is concerned. What people don't know about our secret betrayals of them hurts both them and us.

When we say that nobody else will know if we fail in a trust, we are counting ourselves out of the picture as though our knowledge of ourselves were worthless. But what do we do when we fail ourselves in this particular way? And what is the effect of trying to paper it over as a secret and indifferent activity? We might wonder what we do to ourselves when, even in small things, we violate somebody else's gift of trust. It may be through these seemingly small actions that we begin to cloud our souls and dull our sensitivities. Through such actions we begin the process of hardening our hearts and exiling ourselves from the realm of lasting values. We don't feel that we have done anything wrong, but the price may be that we are less capable of feeling anything in the future.

Breaking a trust involves us in toughening a fibrous and restricting shell around our own existence so that it is harder for us to get out and harder for others to get in. And what, we might also inquire, do we do to those who have trusted us, whether these are our elders, our students, or our friends? When do the hurts show? Perhaps not immediately, perhaps not for a long time, and even then these people who were manipulated or misplayed by us may not be quite sure what happened to them. They may not blame us, but we are the people responsible for their hurt. Things have a way of coming together even after a long time, whether you want to call them chickens coming home to roost or our failures in being trusted making themselves manifest. By whatever name, something real happens and some sure effect takes place in the lives of others when we do not live up to what their trust gives us the chance to be.

We can hardly be faithful people if we are not committed to the two sides of trust. To explore our own reactions to trust leads us more deeply into ourselves than various faddish exercises, body massage, seventeen-day excursions on jet airliners, or the promises of peaceful visions by self-promoting gurus. The territory inside ourselves needs exploration and we can accomplish this, with the aid of the Spirit, on our own. It always seems fearful to begin or to continue a journey that makes us face the truth about ourselves. This trip leads not to some height of sensual experience but to the heart of our own meaning.

This, finally, is what being trusted commits us to—the steady discovery and bringing to light of who we are and what we can be. Faith essentially awakens us to possibilities but making good on them will also make us breathless. The best part of taking trust seriously is not that it delivers unfettered freedom to us but that it does make us aware of the meaning of life. Being trusted means being active rather than passive. It helps us hear the music of our own wonder. So the question is not, Why don't others trust me? but rather, What am I like when I am trusted?

CHAPTER 24

❖

A Way of Looking at Ourselves

Openness includes our basic attitude toward our own personalities. The beginning of wisdom may lie in an unhurried talent for looking at ourselves and not being afraid of what we find. This is precisely what openness—even in small amounts—permits us to do. Instead of seeing ourselves in a stereotyped, distorted, or highly defended fashion, we can also become acquainted with our own possibilities, our unknown strengths and unrealized talents. Openness is a way of making our own growth possible, of keeping away a crabbed and lonely old age, of looking life in the eye and coming up with the response that is new and appropriate even if it is not perfect. We are filled with unsuspected resources; everybody is telling us this, but only openness makes it possible for us ever to see and bring any of these to the surface.

Openness toward ourselves enables us to give our own prejudices and other distorted contents a good airing now and then. What is good for a house that has been shuttered is good for a person who has been closed off. Openness does just this. It makes the contents of our psyche less frightening and enables us to accept and deal with who we are far more realistically and compassionately. Openness frees us the way a brisk walk in the fresh air frees us from the staleness of too much living in a closed-off space.

When we are open to ourselves we find that we are free from being defensive about our faults or shortcomings, that we can even face and begin to deal with our own inclinations to evil. It is not something we can just think about or put into the categories that certain thinkers provide for us. We can only deal with it head-on, tasting the bitterness of our own betrayals of ourselves and others, charting our own tendencies toward selfishness without disguising or denying them.

Being open, in other words, enables us to get a practical sense of what it means to be sinful, a common-sense view of the closed-off soul, the one that has room neither for its own best self nor for anyone else. It can only feast selfishly on life and feel empty at the same time. Openness does not reward us with some romantic view of total goodness within ourselves; it braces us for a mature acceptance of our possibilities for badness as well as for good. A mature person does not enter very deeply into life without some appreciation of this.

Being open means that we are available to life, that we have not shut ourselves off from it in some stifling attic of our own concerns. Openness permits us the greatest of human experiences, to be present in a real way in the lives of others. This deepens our contacts and makes us more aware of life because it provides the nourishment of human sharing that is the raw material of an enlightened spiritual existence.

Revelation is processed through our exchanges with other persons; we give one another the light we need to see ourselves and each other more clearly. That light comes from the openness that permits others to see inside us because we are willing to see out.

A person who is open to life never becomes bored by it,

never thinks that he or she has seen everything or heard everything, or that there is nothing left to learn. Openness enables us to live in time rather than to be left with the desperate choice of passing or killing time.

It has long been known that there are factors within us— aspects of our personalities—that strongly influence the way we look at persons and events around us. Psychological reality consists of a blend of our outer and inner environments. We see things, as the old saying tells us, not necessarily as they are but certainly as we are. Our own needs, prejudices, and fears impose a structure on the world so that we see it the way we want to—or, perhaps more often, the way we must. If we are open to learning more about ourselves, a look into our own eyes tells us something of the personality factors prominent in our habitual way of putting our world together.

To look on the universe with an a priori conviction that it is no good necessarily makes it a forbidding place in which we will be very careful where we step. It may also make us unnecessarily suspicious of other persons and cause us to withdraw too much within ourselves. When we look around and cannot see anything worthwhile it may be because of ourselves rather than because of people in general. This is also true if we confront life with eyes that lack realistic judgment because they have never taken a hard look at our own capacity for evil. Life is not a fixed game but it is not a child's garden of verses either. Somewhere in between these extremes we must adjust our vision so that we are neither mindless in our optimism or overcome by our self-inflicted despair. It is a lifelong task to be open to seeing people and events fairly and as they are rather than as we are.

An immature demand for forced self-disclosure: Openness seems to be defined this way in some current fads of a psychological and spiritual nature. By its very nature, openness is something that comes from inside us. We cannot break into other persons the way we might break into a house in search of treasure. Forcing an awkward openness throws things out of balance and causes people to meet under false conditions that do not last very long.

Telling everybody everything: Some people, infatuated with the idea of openness as a way of life, feel that it means that no thought or feeling should ever be experienced that is not expressed directly and sometimes forcefully to other persons. For them, confrontation is everything and no slight or injury can be allowed to pass unless it is challenged directly. This is a very naive way to live. Persons who want to love learn to forgive and to overlook as many things in others as they wish others would overlook in them. This is not being closed; rather, it means that we are open enough to understand and accept the foibles of others without feeling that we must publicly resent or correct them immediately.

Thinking we must feel and be the same with everybody around us: Openness means we are available to others but life tells us that we are going to have different kinds of friends and varied responses to the persons around us. Some friends are closer than others, and the idea that we can be on the same intimate plane with everybody is unrealistic and destructive of genuine relationships. Communes stumble and finally collapse completely because of this misunderstanding of openness.

CHAPTER 25

Bigheartedness

Do you remember the old bit of doggerel, "If you want a good time, give something away?" The words are as true as ever; joy is the possession of bighearted persons. A lot of giving, unfortunately, is under pressure; we give until it hurts and whether we like it or not. It is not surprising that such compelled giving despoils it of joy.

We can give for many reasons, out of a pinched soul as well as from a large heart. We have no choice about taxes and sometimes not much greater freedom about charitable donations, wedding presents, and a whole long list of other things. Something happens to us, however, when we are overmanipulated into giving, something we should try to lay hold of again. It is the secret of bigheartedness. Our main problem in freeing ourselves so that we can be more loving in our gifts comes to this:

We give out of shame, out of the social pressure that would embarrass us in the eyes of others if we did not give. Other elements also enter in, such as the kind of competition that makes us want to outdo rather than just keep up with our neighbors and the making of pledges and promises because we are afraid not to do so. It is also under this rubric that we give in order to get other people to like us, bargaining for friendship and running the risk of being hypocritical and unnatural at the same time. I once knew an old bishop who would give his episcopal ring away even to relatively new acquaintances at the drop of a miter. What these people, who were properly awed, did not know was that his excellency had a large supply of inexpensive rings harvested from secondhand jewelry shops for just such occasions. Something of his mixed motives came through in these gifts, however, not because the rings seemed false but because the idea seemed false to many of those who received these gifts. It was too much and too soon. This is the tip-off that the giver is trying to capture rather than respond to friendship.

We can give out of private pressure, to avoid the guilt we would feel if we did not give something away. At times this is done out of a desire for atonement or to make something right that we feel we have done wrong. Whenever this happens it arises primarily from our own inner need. Some people learn how to play very skillfully on the guilt of others; they are able to manipulate this feeling to their own advantage. Perhaps a lot of good is done in this high-pressured way. Avoiding an experience of guilt hardly matches the happiness that is the automatic prize of the cheerful giver.

The main difficulty in these psychologically pressured donations is that ultimately we are doing something for ourselves rather than for others. If we aim to avoid shame or to lessen our guilt we remain self-concerned, locked into our own worlds and still at a distance from the bigheartedness that knows neither force nor reluctance in its giving.

Did you ever have somebody give you something unconditionally, something just for you, with no strings, stipulations, or psychological fine print involved? If you have received such a gift—or many such gifts—then you understand the meaning of bigheartedness and you have something for which you can truly be thankful.

Unself-conscious givers respond to others more than to themselves. They have moved sufficiently outside of their own concerns to be able to see others clearly and distinctly, as separate from themselves. Bighearted people have learned to give up something of themselves in order to make room for other people in their lives. There is no loving—and no generous giving—except by those who have been willing to face down their own selfishness and try to pry open the grasping hand that would close only on their own concerns.

There is no scarcity of bighearted people, of course. In fact, they keep the world going, generating hope in a world that is piled high with the evidence of selfishness. Widows' mites and lovers' sacrifices rekindle the fires of our humanity to reacquaint us with the possibility of love in our lives. Such generosity is found in young love all the time. It is more impressive in love that has been tested through the years by heartbreak, disappointment, and the other hazards of the human situation. Every season is a time to utter a prayer of thanks for people who keep on loving in the face of hurt and discouragement. Without such people we would have surrendered to the dark night of history a long time ago. Their lives reflect understanding, gentleness, and joy.

It is all very well to espouse the notion that the best gift is that of our own person, but how do we translate this into action? How does bigheartedness operate on a practical level? Here are some of the ways in which loving people give themselves away to others. We can, for example, make a gift of—

Our Time: This is especially true of the time we save for ourselves, those few minutes or hours we anticipate as an interval in which to do what we please, shutting the world out for a little justified self-concern. The trouble with giving this time away is that there is no way that one can ever retrieve it. Moments of quiet are difficult to come by; to surrender them means to say farewell to them. That is why this is such a profound way of giving ourselves to others. It takes bighearted persons to give up their time; they are the only ones who ever do.

Our Concern: This includes our attention as well as our interest in other persons. There is a big difference, after all, in claiming to be interested in others and then proving it in a practical manner. It is easy to give a part of our attention to other persons, perhaps even half of it. That is not the same as the full-hearted gift of our informed concern. When we give our attention to others, we make ourselves present to them in a way that is unmistakable. This is, of course, an intangible gift and an invaluable one at the same time.

Our Understanding: This takes us a step beyond attention because through it we make an active effort to enter the world of another person and to comprehend it with appreciation and compassion. Understanding is a rare gift and it is only exchanged between human beings. We need only think of what it means when someone else understands us to realize what a great gift understanding can be when it flows from our own open hearts toward others.

Our Feelings: Our feelings are very private. We can keep them to ourselves and no one is ever the wiser. We can be with others, for example, and seem to be interested in them while, in truth, we are concerned only with our own emotions. Something must die in us if we are to yield up our own feelings for ourselves in order to come fully alive for others. On the practical level, this is one of the most demanding yet most effective ways we have of giving ourselves away.

Our Spirit: This is something we give even when we do not know it. It is the gift that is always available to those around us when we are involved in life in an active and purposeful way. People can receive this present from us without taking anything away from us. We are not, in fact, diminished by any of these gifts of our true selves. We are only enlarged. The word "magnanimous" comes from the Latin words meaning great-souled or great-spirited. That is the word which we translate ordinarily as bighearted. It means that the availability of our inner selves is the most important mark of our identity.

Perhaps one of the reasons that thank-yous are such a problem is that we are uncertain about our attitudes in the situation. Not only does too much thanks smother us and no thanks at all kill us in another way, but also our thank-yous can reveal to us the heart of our own motivations for helping people in the first place. We can think too much about this subject, there is no doubt of that, and yet, at the risk of excessive introspection, it is healthy to check out our attitudes toward giving and receiving. Somehow, the process of thanking and being thankful puts into focus some of our central attitudes toward other persons, attitudes that show us the depth of our own lives.

The reason for this is our frequent use of favors to lay claim to others; that is to say, we very often do things for others because we want them to like us. Our favors are like mining claims in that we stake out the territory of another personality from which we want to extract the riches of their attention and affection. Other people's thank-yous become important to us as a sign that they recognize the special nature of our relationship to them. We are not just anybody to them; we are somebody special, and we like to warm ourselves with that glowing feeling. Some of this may exist in all our relationships, but these relationships will never get deeper until we can purge ourselves of this motivation, until, in other words, we can shift the balance of payments so that we begin to love the other for his or her sake rather than just for our own. For most of us, this is a lifelong process, and we should not be discouraged to find that we still have much work to do in this regard. We cannot ignore the subtleties in the journeys of our hearts, however, and examining our attitudes toward the gratitude of others is as good a place to begin as we are likely to find.

CHAPTER 26

———————◆———————

Things That Work,
Things That Don't

Some advance has been made in the world's realization that not all change, even when labeled progress, represents improvement. For example, an article in the New York *Times Magazine* developed a rationale for why things usually don't work very well. The example cited was the Aswan Dam, that expensive project designed to generate energy in Egypt. It turns out that the dam has interfered with the Nile River's depositing silt, that rich fertilizer, on its course to the sea, resulting in harm to farm production. A good deal of the energy generated by the dam must be used now to develop fertilizer to replace that which it caused to disappear in the first place.

One could multiply examples from public life, including plastic clothes, most frozen foods, and the superhighways that slice cities into ribbons, but perhaps we could all find private examples that would be just as telling. One of the most ancient temptations is to make resolutions about how we are going to improve ourselves in the next year. Here we might be wise to follow the old adage, "If it works, don't fix it." This also applies in our personal lives, and for a very simple reason.

It takes a long time to get used to each other, and the

lessons of relationship are as complex and hard to master as the design of snowflakes. People communicate on a variety of levels and they grow accustomed to signals that are exchanged subtly and in silence as well as those that are more obvious and uttered aloud. So the heart always has reasons that reason by itself will never understand, and this applies equally between spouses and between friends. When people who love each other reach some way of saying what they want—and what they need—to express, they should not tamper lightly with it. Don't interfere with love or friendship that works; don't try to fix it or, of all things, improve it.

But there are those tempted to improve it, tempted by some new book or fad, some new method that demands "being honest" in a way that proves ultimately more disruptive than helpful. The heart can never be seized by force, and hardly any of the improvements suggested by others can enlarge the intimacy we have achieved in the only way possible, slowly and surely and in accord with a rhythm that may be out of synchronization with the age but not with the abiding demands of human relationships.

Sometimes people who love each other take a long way around to say something important to each other; sometimes the weightiest of sentiments is conveyed by the lightest of touches, the largest themes of love are expressed in the smallest symbols and gestures. Better that truly loving people follow their instincts in these things than that they try radically or dramatically to change.

Since when has bluntness been an improvement on sensitivity, or confrontation an advance on tenderness? The best of life's lessons are learned uniquely, and at very close range; sometimes the essence of this learning cannot be explained or passed on to others. It can only be respected, as

one respects the nature of rivers as carriers of nourishment
for the next season's harvest. In matters of the heart, hesitate before you attempt major improvements that might
destroy what you think you are enlarging. The happiness
you save may be your own.

CHAPTER 27

—————◆—————

How Much Truth Is Enough?

What about being truthful? After all, we do not live our lives in a courtroom in which we are bound to tell the truth, the whole truth, and nothing but the truth. Nobody is going to arrest us for perjury for a little white lie or we would all be in jail by nightfall. And there are those who say that even people who love each other very much need not tell each other everything. I had a wise old professor once who, in confidential and earnest tones, would say to us, "Tell the truth . . . but not too much!" Well, how much truth is enough?

We must face and share the truth that defines us in what we really mean to ourselves and to others. That leaves plenty of room for not hurting others' feelings needlessly and it also makes a clearing in the soul where fidelity to ourselves can take root and grow. There is a living and invisible force that is generated by faithfulness within ourselves that weathers and strengthens us like a warming sun. This is the heart of stable truth about ourselves which others can touch and sense as reliable and trustworthy. It is the rock on which our identity rests and its outlines can be seen even through the light mist of exaggeration or the heavier weather of an occasional self-administered snow job. We have to hold on to that fundamental truth that springs from a good sense of ourselves or we cannot even recognize, much less share who we are with anybody else.

There is a tension connected with keeping up with the truth about ourselves; this is because we are constantly having new experiences that we must face and name accurately in order to incorporate them into ourselves. Of course, this is simple enough with relatively easy things like disappointment when our favorite team loses or excitement at the arrival of good news. It is more complicated when we must keep up with the subtle and hard-to-name emotions that can arise in the course of friendship or love. It is difficult for a person to mark down jealousy as a feeling of his own, or to accept and label a hurt unwittingly inflicted by another. These are the very truths, however, which must be met head-on rather than denied. Each of them has a meaning that we must uncover if we are to keep our relationships loving and true.

Love can face hard truths and survive quite well; it has a terrible time, however, when it is denied the truth or is misled in some way or other. This is the "not enough truth" that kills friendship and love the way a boa constrictor does its victims—by a long, steady, suffocating pressure. People who are caught in this never can quite remember where things started going wrong; they can only look back after they know that things are, in fact, very wrong and they do not know how to put them right again.

Enough truth means that we know what is happening to us in our relationship with another and that we are willing to communicate that as clearly and sensitively as possible. Enough truth means that faithfulness to ourselves if functional and central in our experiences. Enough truth means that we are not afraid of what is real about ourselves and that we can face it without distorting it too much in order to make it more attractive. Enough truth means that we meet each other with our own voices and our own words and that we never give up trying to express, even a little at a time, our own truths to each other.

CHAPTER 28

——◆——

Turning Points

Where are the turning points in life? It is easy enough to
see them as we look backward; we say, sometimes sadly
and sometimes happily, that this or that event made all the
difference. But they are very difficult—almost impossible—
to see as we approach them. They are, in fact, hard to make
out clearly even when we are in the midst of them. Yet
there would be more than a small advantage in being able
to read life's turning points more sensitively: pain to save
and heartbreak to avoid, better decisions to be made and a
fuller use of ourselves in life. Can we learn to discern the
geography of our growth and development more accurately? Can we even learn to admit the important turning
points and so live with them more realistically and perhaps
more peacefully? If it were easy we would already be doing
it.

There are natural turning points—graduation, job
changes, moves to other parts of the country, getting married, starting a family. All of these are clearly junctions
which, once crossed, find us changed for good. But there
are other moments, more subtle, yes, but just as irreversible
in their consequences. Think of the magic, never found in
life, but part of every fairy tale—"They lived happily ever
after." That sunlit and spacious time never comes for any
of us.

We speak, however, of other and quite similar times, of the moments after which "things were never quite the same," or the incidents after which "things began to go better," or, sadly, after which things "never quite went well." Perhaps these quiet passages, as unmarked as the sea after a ship has passed, are the times we should inspect, both for what they tell us about our lives and ourselves and for the wisdom they can give us to live more fully in the future.

The trouble with these dividing lines is that they can only be drawn as an outcome of growth. What gives them substance is the living that precedes them, the choices, some of them large and solemn but most of them seemingly incidental, teased from the sheerest of the material of life, and others that appear more accidental than anything else. These all coalesce with a force and strength of their own, the distillate of our personality accumulating without our noticing it, but giving an unexpected shape to our lives.

We forge our destinies in such silent times, when it does not seem to matter so much but when, in fact, we are drawing, to small but exact scale, the directions for our future lives. We call it good or bad luck only later on; we find names like fate or think that it was all written in the stars, when it was actually something we were fashioning all the while.

The turning points of life follow a mass of such choices; there is a logic to them that we cannot escape. Our providence is far more under our control than we sometimes allow ourselves to think. A better future is our inheritance when we can observe ourselves while we are so quietly doing the things that are finally so important. It is something like a good marriage or raising a good family. They are the outcome of the thousand seemingly nameless choices that go with sacrifice and sensitivity, with a sense that the things of everyday are the only elements that hold any hint of the things that last forever.

CHAPTER 29

———◆———

Meeting a Good Person

We meet good people all the time, but in the rush of life we sometimes do not recognize them or look closely enough to realize how their goodness also offers us a sign of what we can yet become ourselves. They are givers of hope, these good people who stand all around us. I felt this recently when I met a salesman whom I had not seen in several months. I had not known that in the meantime this gentle and good man had suffered a stroke and was just now getting back to work. As he stood there, the worn spots on his overcoat showing and his clothes now a couple of sizes too large, he did not look like a sick person as much as a noble one. I could somehow sense in him the human person's capacity to fight back against hardship and pain; something of the great dignity of a good person stood out in him. He did not make much of his illness, although he mentioned how discouraging it was not to feel quite like himself yet. He was a man fighting back, not feeling sorry for himself, and not yielding anything to the odds that serious illness had piled up against him. Despite his graying hair and his lined and drawn face, he was a heroic figure, a man full of simple human promise who preached a better sermon than most of the ones I have heard in my life. It was, of course, the sermon of renewed life triumphing over old difficulties, the refreshing message of what a real man can be. The wonder is that such people can be found everywhere; each one tells a different story of renewed life, each one has the gifts of hope and promise for us if we only look at them.

Meeting ourselves again also happens all the time but not necessarily when we are looking at that distorted view we have of ourselves in the mirror, or when we are trying to make a good impression, or when we attempt to disguise our small failings. Those are occasions when, if anything, we turn away from ourselves. We feel more comfortable, of course, when we don't have to tally up our debts or cost-account our failures with merciless accuracy. We seldom think, however, to look on the credit side, perhaps because our improvements have been slow and not as numerous as our faults sometimes seem to be. What is good—what has changed for the better about us—is proof to ourselves that we have come to grips with ourselves and overcome old problems with new and more creative responses. There is more to us, in other words, than we may ordinarily give ourselves credit for. Covering ourselves up, whether with distorting styles, makeup, or the special armor of psychological defensiveness, may make us miss what is best and most promising about us—the truth that God gives us strength to enlarge our lives.

CHAPTER 30

Things We've Got Backward

It is bad enough to try to live by aphorisms, but it is intolerable to live by clichés. And aphorisms, even those of the great Dr. Franklin, grow slowly but surely into clichés, reversing somewhat the transformation of the grain of sand into the shiny pearl. Indeed, the pearls of one year's slogans gradually lose their luster and change from minor glories of wisdom into pebbles in our shoes.

And the fact is that many of the sayings that are endlessly quoted, printed on posters, and stitched into banners are wrong or at least misleading. Think of some of our most famous ones; think, if you will, of one that we will hear quoted frequently during any political campaign—Franklin Roosevelt's "The only thing we have to fear is fear itself." Now, do you really believe that? It sounds good if you don't think too much about it, and maybe that is the kind of slogan that was needed in a depression-struck country; but it does not really bear careful examination.

As a matter of fact, there are plenty of things to be afraid of—from nuclear war to the flu—and anybody who doesn't understand this is in for a great deal of trouble. Those who think that there are not readily recognizable dangers around us or who think that fear is some kind of betrayal of our macho ideal make themselves twice vulnerable. Only those who sense and understand their fear can do something about discovering its source and doing something about it. Fear is informative and we should read its messages carefully if we are concerned about our survival and the survival of coming generations. If we don't allow ourselves to experience healthy fear, we choose a naive and foolhardy position, one that invites every invented demon to explain our bad luck or travail, a situation in which we make fate the master of existence and its handmaid, panic, the companion of our darker days. The only thing we really have to fear is the idea that there is nothing to fear but fear itself.

But wait a moment. Consider a great favorite, one that captures the heady optimism of booster America, the phrase of Rotarian theology. "Today is the first day of the rest of your life." It is okay, you say, and what if it is less than profound? Well, perhaps the problem is that it slices away our past as though its energies had no meaning nor way of entrance into our future. It wipes away the bad of our personal histories, but it may erase much of what is solid and good at the same time. We never address ourselves successfully to the future unless we have a feeling for the past, which may have been prologue but which remains with us in important ways.

The slogan needs reworking. It makes more sense to say, "Today is the last day of the first of your life." We have been somewhere and we have the scars to prove it; we are our past and we cannot disown it or wish it away. Wisdom, yes, and real faith turn us to the future with respect for the journey we have already made and with a sense that, as we have kept faith with our origins and traditions, so we can enter tomorrow, or begin again, or start fresh at life. Deep faith assures us not that we can reach impossible goals but the ones that are truly possible for us in view of our gifts and achievements. We are always ending the first part of our life; that is what convinces us that the best is yet to come.

Examine, if you will, another favorite that has been incorporated into wedding ceremonies, sermons, and banners beyond number: "Let there be spaces in your togetherness." Now, there is a real meaning here, to be sure, but we may have overemphasized it in the self-centered age through which we have been passing. Isolation and distance have their place, but they are not complete ideals. Perhaps we should rephrase this saying as well. It makes better contemporary sense if it reads, "Let there be bridges in your togetherness." If there is one thing that modern persons may need assistance with, it is in breaking out of their own shells and learning how to reach each other in a genuine way. The spaces in our togetherness will be there anyway; we won't have to create any new ones because we will be busy enough respecting those that are already there. But reaching out of our shells and touching others with tenderness and concern—this is a matter of the highest importance, the truth of intimacy that many have forgotten or never learned.

There are too many spaces in what we call togetherness, too many evidences of an almost impacted selfishness in what writer Tom Wolfe has dubbed "The Me Decade." There are too many people marrying projections of themselves, phantoms generated by their own needs, and they are not at all in touch with the real person of their spouse. Their togetherness is all space, and they are oppressed by the discovery that they do not know and sometimes do not even like very much the one they married. No, it is time to again learn to build bridges of relationship and to retire the slogan that can be interpreted to exalt separateness too much.

The all-time favorite, of course, must be that shallow paragraph of the late psychologist Fritz Perls, reproduced here in its entirety: "I do my thing and you do your thing. I am not in this world to live up to your expectations and you are not in this world to live up to mine. You are you and I am I and if by chance we find each other, it's beautiful."

Well, maybe it is beautiful, but life cannot be lived successfully as an accidental affair, something like a roller derby in which the skaters are doing their thing with intense self-absorption, pleasing themselves and to hell with anybody else, and if there is a collision that sends a couple into each other's arms for a few moments, well, that's beautiful.

The basic problem here is that what Perls said appeals to something immature in us, a desire for a freedom uncompromised by responsibility, to a romantic and finally unsupportable individualism that is far more stark and lonely than the revered legends of the lone cowboy heading out of town on his own again at the end of the story or the film. But let us examine it phrase by phrase.

"I do my thing and you do your thing." Yes, but where do we do these "things"? In some vacuum, in spheres so distinct that we never meet, cross each other's path, or need somebody else's help? The fact is that part of doing our "thing" is learning to do it in relationship to others and with respect for them and for their rights and interests. Not even the most remote artist or poet can pretend to total independence in pursuing a vision of art. We are involved with each other and, while that chafes at times, it is through working out all the complexities in an interrelated universe that meaning is delivered to any of our achievements.

"I am not in this world to live up to your expectations . . ." No, perhaps not, but there is nothing intrinsically wrong with meeting sensible expectations placed on us by others. Indeed, it is important for us as parents, teachers, preachers, or spouses to have some expectations on the behavior of others and not apologize constantly for having them. We cripple people when we do not raise expectations, we destroy any possibility of excellence and we obscure some of life's most significant sources of meaning.

Any number of experiments have demonstrated the role of healthy expectation in assisting persons to develop to their fullest. It is an empty desert of a world stripped of all directional signs and goals when we fail to acknowledge the role of expectation in our existence. Hope is the child of healthy expectation and love comes to life in the next generation. Expectation as investment of the self in others is essential to any human and properly spiritual understanding of our lives.

The last of these slogans is the saddest of all because it exalts isolation and despises rightful claims. It sounds good to the unthinking, but such a set of attitudes, narcissistic in each layer, is the death of everything that makes existence truly beautiful. So it may be time to retire some of these clichés, to haul down the banners that have stared us down so long, and return to something simpler and grander—common sense and traditional values about what we mean to each other.

CHAPTER 31

———◆———

What Comes to an End?

There is an end to childhood, we know, and an end to innocence as well. They are related events, overlapping experiences that are sometimes confusing and dismaying. It is hard to give up any stage of adjustment in our lives. And yet growth seems to demand that we do this all the time.

Sometimes we do not know what has ended in our lives until a long time later, or when we are at a sufficient distance to be able to see it in better perspective. We look and say, "I didn't know it then but that was the last time I would ever be that free . . . or that healthy . . . or that sad . . . or that much in love. . . ."

We might long for what seems now to be the sun-filled days of childhood, but we realize that they had to end and that we had to change. We look back to times when we thought life had ended because of some transformation or some loss. But life ends only if we refuse to let some part of it end. It crumbles only when we reject the mystery of ending that confronts us almost every day. We may not be able to run out to meet them, but we can accept and open ourselves to the endings, almost beyond counting, that fall, like a long series of crossing gates, across our paths.

If we think about the things we postpone—the big things, that is—we find that they are often connected with an ending we do not want to face, an ending either for ourselves or others. We put off saying good-bye in a thousand scenes we hate to leave. We hesitate to break bad news or to come to terms with a difficult truth that might threaten our relationship with somebody else—that might alter it or bring it to a complete end.

We leave things undone because we sometimes prefer loose ends to closed doors, situations that are bad to those that get worse. We want to avoid the finality of endings and to preserve the illusion that things haven't changed, that they are just the way they have always been.

And yet things change on us even as we try to hold them together. Endings multiply, and unless we can make peace with this truth we end up living in dreams, our lives filled with unfulfilled hopes and worn-out loves, our hearts turned into attics so filled with things we cannot let go of that there is no room for anything fresh and new. When we cannot manage the endings of our lives we rule out any new beginnings. We kill hope because we have no real faith, nothing to allow us to see the seeds of what is to come in the ashes of the things that are over.

"Bittersweet" is a word for endings. We all have mixed feelings about them; that is why they are hard to face and deal with. Wise therapists, for example, understand that as the hour of treatment draws to a close, very important material may be discussed by patients even in casual and seemingly offhanded ways. We cannot help but react to the pressure of an important hour's ending because, whether we like it or even acknowledge it, it stirs the memories of all the important separations and good-byes of our lives. An ending may touch a live wire in our psyche that we have gingerly stepped over for a long time. And there we are, feeling again the tearing of the self that goes with lovers parting, children growing up and growing away, and death itself, like an elusive workman loosening the moorings of our souls each time we lose a friend or a loved one to him.

Endings are an aspect of the mystery that is at work in us all the time. Look away from it and it does not vanish; face it and we enter more deeply into our lives and we possess our souls in a new way. It is not strange that we have mixed feelings about the things that constantly come to an end in our presence. It is only strange that we do not recognize how mixed most of our feelings always are in the human situation, how hard it is to let go and open our hands and lives to something new. Uneasiness is the natural state of the growing person; it is what we are bound to feel, even the most noble-hearted among us, when we taste the mystery of separation.

We need to take time in order to see the meaning of endings in our own lives. It is not a clear and simple experience; the scythe of separation all too often seems to have a dull and rusty cutting edge. We face our ambivalence at every turn, and even when we are fairly grown up we may not be safe from the burden of mixed feelings.

There are so many things we want to see end, and then, oddly, we miss them when they do, the way soldiers miss the excitement and seeming purposefulness of war. We think back to more difficult times—times we prayed would end perhaps—and find that we have lost something good in the discipline we had to acquire in order to survive them. Lovers think back to times when they had nothing or when they could see each other rarely or for short periods and they know that a special happiness went with all those painful separations and good-byes.

And how many things there are that we think we do not want to see end—holidays, summer evenings, a sweet moment of peace with friends. But there is no escaping these endings without destroying the pattern of experience that gives them heightened meaning in the first place. Indeed, much of our life is built on being able to live under a changing sky or within the crushing limits of time. Because things have endings we can see their shape more clearly. Believing allows us to see beyond our everyday endings to what lies beyond them. It involves us in the future, in always being born again, in the joy of understanding that no ending of life is a final ending. We can also understand that the things that give us the courage to face the deaths of our thousand yearly endings are the very qualities that last and carry us into the future.

Something in us, of course, wants always to clutch at the moment or at whatever possessions are ours. Indeed, one of the greatest frustrations human beings experience is their inability to enjoy fully the things that they have worked so hard to own. There are many rueful glances these days at faded American dreams, at the house in the suburbs, the use of leisure in travel, the explosion of things to spend money on and enjoy.

How common it is for persons to feel empty at the very moment in which they think they are filled with the things they have always wanted. They cannot quite close their hands on them, or invade them, or comfort themselves with them in the way they had hoped. Frequently their possessions—honest and decent ones—become a burden they feel they will have to carry endlessly.

There is a special kind of ending to this sort of having. We call it a limitation, a recognition that nothing we own or hide away exists independent of the restrictions. There is an edge to everything, a wall beyond which we cannot travel, a barrier which, despite wealth and power, we cannot overcome. Only those people with a sense of life's limits have any chance at peace or happiness.

Seizing the moment is fine but holding on to it forever is impossible and self-destructive. That is why the philosophies of pleasure that deny limits and camouflage endings are so deceptive and, in the long run, so dispiriting. The current effort to treat sex, for example, solely as a pleasurable activity—sex as entertainment—tears it out of its human context and makes it more difficult for persons to see deeply into its meaning. How can people sense the significance of what poets have for so long called the "little death" that is involved in profound sexual sharing if their ideal makes no room for limitations? How many persons count themselves inadequate or as failures when they are really only human? How much richer is all human activity when persons have an operational sense of their own limits.

The things without endings are few and they are spiritual in nature. They hint at all that lies beyond our limitations. We touch them, conditioned still by our humanity, when somebody believes in, or trusts us, or loves us freely and generously. There is no limitation on real love; it is only false or inadequate love that is under threat by time or separation. Real love finds its test in what seem to be endings—in good-byes, in forced separations, and in all the patient waiting of the world's lovers. Endings awaken us to the areas of life which they do not destroy; they help us to achieve a new depth of self and relationship with others. Good people who have the power to give life in small ways bring a bigger meaning to themselves and to everyone around them. We just need to be reminded of the power of renewal that is ours whenever we reach out to people around us. Our biggest danger lies in forgetting that we can give life to others and make it larger and more beautiful—

even if only in simple and seemingly unremarkable ways. As the poet Alice Duer Miller wrote:

> If ever I said, in grief or pride,
> I tired of honest things, I lied.

We are without faith if we think we do not have an effect on the balance of things. Loving people keep the whole universe in the balance. But how?

By refusing to return to adolescence once they have come close to being adults. The temptation is surely there, made more appealing by the promises of eternal youth, fashionableness, and the applause of those around us. The country long ago got over its need for a good five-cent cigar. It has never quite appreciated, though, its need for adults who are at peace with themselves and who do not try to recross the border into late adolescence in order to be popular or feel self-assured. Mature adults, without even trying hard, automatically help younger people to move toward adulthood. Grown-ups provide a goal that activates the guidance systems of young people toward maturity.

Adults give life when, for example, they are still capable of saying no to others, when, in other words, they are not intimidated out of one of their most sensible functions, providing reasonable boundaries for growing people. "No" does not have to come from a mean-spirited, fun-killing person who has forgotten what it means to be young. A "no" can flow from a loving and responsible judgment, from, in other words, some genuine caring for other persons. And so it does not necessarily mean a desperate overcontrol of another's destiny; mature limits actually build an individual's capacity for freedom because they educate persons to the meaning of choice and the relative good of various situations.

Adults generate life in others when they display a sense of self-discipline about themselves, when, in other words, they can say no to themselves as well as to others. We live in a time in which the praiseworthy goal of self-fulfillment has been dangerously equated with impulsive selfishness. People can walk away from family, children, and other commitments to "find life" for themselves without much concern for the death this may deal to others. In a current book, *Mama Doesn't Live Here Anymore,* author Judy Sullivan describes how she left her husband and eleven-year-old daughter saying, "I can't take care of anyone else," and that she wanted to have "full responsibility for my own life." New York *Times* critic Anatole Broyard, reflecting on the book, touches the nerve of why so many adults cannot give life to others: "The final picture of the author is one of infantile narcissism: doing exactly what she wants to do whenever she wants to do it." There may be nothing as old-fashioned sounding as self-sacrifice or self-discipline, but they are indispensable to us if we hope to make a difference in the lives of others.

We can also be consistent in our attitudes and in our actions. Being a whole person is evidenced in the integrity of our presence in life. It doesn't mean that we can never change or that we are fated to a rigid conservatism; it suggests, rather, that we fit together as persons and that we live by principle rather than whim, by conviction rather than impulse. Some say that the disclosures about lying and manipulation in government are nothing new and that we should make cynical peace with this reality—a momentarily comforting argument at best that makes the cure for failed integrity worse than the problem. We give life, however, when we live truthfully, with well-thought-out convictions rather than with slogans or fads, when we fit together with the wholeness that is the basis for holiness.

We give life when we know the difference between authority and authoritarianism, when we take ourselves seriously enough to know that life is not a random proposition and that nothing we do is ever small enough not to have an impact on others. Authority, as I have often noted, comes from a word signifying "to make able to grow" rather than "to control." Being in a relationship in which we have responsibility for the growth of others demands more from us than just keeping things in good order. This is why writers are called *authors* and why they have a special relationship to their words and works.

This is the kind of relationship parents have with their children, teachers with their students, religious leaders with their people. Helping persons grow recommits us to a life-giving stance in their regard. It is a continuing journey, never carried out abstractly or through manipulation. We only achieve it if we are there, the best we can manage, with a vision of the possibilities for good that are always available to us. We may live far from the scandals and disasters or the great movers and shakers who represent power in this world. But the power of loving people has always been a different sort; it is that which, unlike the thirst for power, is patient and kind, never jealous or conceited. It delights in the truth, and, best of all, it does not come to an end.